RED SCARE

COMMUNISTS IN AMERICA

PUBLIC PERSECUTIONS   Budd Bailey

Cavendish
Square
New York

Published in 2017 by Cavendish Square Publishing, LLC
243 5th Avenue, Suite 136, New York, NY 10016

Library of Congress Cataloging-in-Publication Data

Names: Bailey, Budd, 1955- author.
Title: Red scare : communists in America / Budd Bailey.
Description: New York : Cavendish Square Publishing, [2017] | Series: Public
persecutions | Includes bibliographical references and index.
Identifiers: LCCN 2016025097 (print) | LCCN 2016027247 (ebook) | ISBN
9781502623256 (library bound) | ISBN 9781502623263 (E-book)
Subjects: LCSH: Anti-communist movements–United States–History–20th
century. | McCarthy, Joseph, 1908-1957. | Cold War–Social aspects–United
States. | United States–Politics and government–20th century.
Classification: LCC E743.5 .B25 2017 (print) | LCC E743.5 (ebook) | DDC
973.921092–dc23
LC record available at https://lccn.loc.gov/2016025097

Editorial Director: David McNamara
Editor: Fletcher Doyle
Copy Editor: Nathan Heidelberger
Associate Art Director: Amy Greenan
Designer: Stephanie Flecha
Production Coordinator: Karol Szymczuk
Photo Research: J8 Media

The photographs in this book are used by permission and through the courtesy of:
Cover Universal History Archive/UIG via Getty Images; p. 4 Bettmann/Getty Images; p. 6 Bettmann/Getty Images; p. 8 Universal
History Archive/Getty Images; p. 13 Library of Congress/Corbis/VCG via Getty Images; p. 16 Bettmann/Getty Images ; p. 20
NY Daily News Archive via Getty Images; p. 23 Bettmann/Getty Images; p. 28 Bettmann/Getty Images; p. 32 Keystone/Getty
Images; p. 36 AP Photo; p. 39 Universal History Archive/Getty Images; p. 43 AP Photo; p. 45 Photo12/UIG via Getty Images;
p. 51 Bettmann/Getty Images; p. 54 U.S. Air Force/File:C-47s at Tempelhof Airport Berlin 1948.jpg/Wikimedia Commons; p.
56 AP Photo/WCA; p. 61 Bettmann/Getty Images; p. 69 Walter Bennett/The LIFE Picture Collection/Getty Images; p. 73 Roger
Higgins, photographer from "New York World-Telegram and the Sun"/File:Julius and Ethel Rosenberg NYWTS.jpg/Wikimedia
Commons; p. 79 Bettmann/Getty Images; p. 81 Bettmann/Getty Images; p. 83 Bettmann/Getty Images; p. 86 Bettmann/Getty
Images; p. 89 John Springer Collection/CORBIS/Corbis via Getty Images; p. 92 Hank Walker/The LIFE Picture Collection/Getty
Images; p. 95 Bettmann/Getty Images; p. 98 Ed Clark/The LIFE Picture Collection/Getty Images; p. 103 A. W. Cox/Central Press/
Hulton Archive/Getty Images; p. 107 Lisa Larsen/The LIFE Images Collection/Getty Images; p. 109 Aleks49/Shutterstock.com.

Printed in the United States of America

Contents

Suppressing Civil Liberties

The First Amendment to the United States Constitution reads as follows:

> Congress shall make no law respecting an establishment of religion, or prohibiting the free exercise thereof; or abridging the freedom of speech, or of the press; or the right of the people peaceably to assemble, and to petition the Government for a redress of grievances.

Those few words have been at the heart of the discussion surrounding Communists who have lived and worked in the United States.

A good-sized part of the issue is that free speech is not an absolute right in all situations. The Supreme Court has handed down several rulings on this issue. The most famous of the decisions came in *Schenck v. United States* in 1918. In the unanimous decision, Justice Oliver Wendell Holmes Jr. wrote, "The most stringent protection of free speech would not

Opposite: Supreme Court Justice Oliver Wendell Holmes Jr. wrote a landmark legal opinion on free speech, one of several that put restrictions on speech.

Demonstrators display their sympathies toward Communism in a rally in the United States around 1920.

protect a man in falsely shouting fire in a theatre and causing a panic." The court also has ruled on restrictions on speech over such areas as lies, obscenities, and inciting violence, as well as laws governing statements by government employees.

There have been a variety of opinions on the issue. Some people believe that any sort of speech should be allowed, while others think that restrictions are often necessary. And that brings us to the question of Communists in America, a subject the US has dwelt on for about a century.

Communism, as practiced in the Soviet Union from 1917 to 1991, is a political and economic system that believes the government, not people and private companies, should own businesses, property, and resources. In theory, classes do not exist in Communism—everyone is roughly equal. There is only one political party, so there are no direct elections of leaders. That theory is in direct contrast to the United States, which uses capitalism. That's an economic system in which the people own businesses, resources, and property. This is not an either/or question; such systems fall on a spectrum. For example, **Socialism** as practiced in certain countries has elements of both Communism and capitalism.

Over the years, Communists tried to export their philosophy to the United States. Some would have supported violent methods to achieve that goal, while others preferred persuasion through legal means. Communism never took hold in America, but that doesn't mean Americans weren't nervous about the idea. Many laws were passed to restrict the activities of Communists. Were these laws necessary or appropriate? That's where the arguments begin.

There's no debate that Communists have suffered some degree of persecution over the past century. It's been subtle, without many imprisonments or executions. But Communists certainly lost some of the rights guaranteed to them in the United States Constitution.

Arguments about issues such as freedom of speech and freedom of assembly are liable to exist as long as America exists. That's why we study them—we don't know who the next person or group to come under scrutiny will be.

ONE

The First Time

It is late in 1916 in Petrograd—previously known as St. Petersburg—in Russia, and the capital city is in chaos. In a sense, the road to Communism begins here.

Russia had joined with England and France in the fight against Germany and Austria-Hungary when what came to be known as World War I started. Russia was led by **Czar** Nicholas II, who thought he personally could lead his troops to a glorious victory. He was talked out of it but still spent much of his time away from Petrograd. Russia quickly lost early battles despite having the biggest army in the world.

Nicholas's absence meant his wife, Alexandra, ran the Russian government from Petrograd. She wasn't any more suited for that role than her husband was to be a military leader. Alexandra relied on the advice of Rasputin, a shadowy character who wasn't trusted by anyone except the **czarina**.

In October 1916, railroad workers in Petrograd went on strike to protest poor working conditions. Troops were called back from the front to try to restore order, but they soon joined

Opposite: Vladimir Lenin led the overthrow of the Russian government in 1917.

the strikers. By the end of 1916, the Russian population was hungry in spite of a great farm crop. Financial policies by the government had led to strong **inflation**, which meant the price of food had gone up faster than the people's ability to pay for it.

Conditions continued to deteriorate in Russia as 1917 began. On March 8, those waiting in a bread line stormed a bakery, only to have police open fire on the population. That angered the one hundred thousand people who were part of a general strike. When the military was called to quiet the rebellion, the soldiers joined the strikers. Within days, Nicholas had given up the throne and an interim government had taken control.

Lenin Moves In

A man named Vladimir Ilyich Ulyanov, who became better known under the name Vladimir Lenin, was trying to follow developments in Russia from Switzerland. Lenin had been part of an attempt to overthrow the Russian government in 1905 and was exiled to Switzerland.

Lenin had read the published work of Karl Marx and Friedrich Engels, who wrote *The Communist Manifesto* in 1848. Marx and Engels believed that workers would eventually rise up and take away control of businesses, resources, and government from the ruling class. Lenin thought Communism would be well received in the industrialized nations of the world, such as England. However, he changed his mind when Russia, with an economy based on farming, fell into turmoil.

Lenin returned to his native country in dramatic fashion, arriving at Finland Station (a railroad terminal) in Petrograd on April 3, 1917. He had expected to be arrested as soon as he arrived, but instead, supporters were there to welcome him back. "Dear Comrades, soldiers, sailors and workers, I am happy to greet you in the name of the victorious Russian Revolution, to greet you as the advance guard of the international proletarian army," he said.

Lenin was ready to lead his supporters in a battle for control of Russia. The interim government was still at war with Germany and its allies, but its attention was very divided.

Lenin's forces, known as the Bolsheviks, took control of the Russian government in November 1917 and slowly started consolidating their gains. The capital was moved to Moscow in 1918, and Russia quietly withdrew from World War I around the same time. A civil war broke out that lasted a few years, but Lenin's side usually had the upper hand. The first Communist country in world history had been established.

The United States of America noticed the Russian Revolution, of course, mostly because America had entered World War I on the side of the Allies in 1917. Many in the United States weren't happy with Russia's departure from the war, as beating Germany and Austria-Hungary became a more difficult task with its withdrawal. Still, American manpower and materials soon made a difference. What looked like a stalemate in early 1918 quickly turned into a rout. Surrender by Germany and its allies came on November 11, 1918, and "**the war to end all wars**" was over.

Winning wars is never easy, with the loss of life and the other sacrifices by all of those involved. Winning the peace can be difficult, too.

America got off relatively easy in terms of sacrifices, mostly because the fighting took place on European rather than American soil. That didn't mean the war didn't change the country. This was the first time that the United States had fought a major war in Europe, and after the war's conclusion, it was only natural for many Americans to want to close the doors to foreign involvements. This is known as isolationism.

Wilson's Failed Plan

President Woodrow Wilson saw the end of World War I as an opportunity to put in place a grand design for a new and improved world order. "The world must be made safe for democracy," Wilson argued. His **Fourteen Points** plan was designed for that purpose. But it turned out to be a rather idealistic proposal. America's allies—England, France, and Italy—were more interested in handing out harsh punishment to the defeated countries than they were in spreading democracy. The result was a peace treaty that left bitterness among defeated nations and set the stage for another worldwide conflict about twenty years later.

As for America, one of the cornerstones of Wilson's plan was to form a League of Nations. The idea was for representatives from the world's countries to gather in one place in an attempt to settle their differences peacefully. Opponents to the plan believed that America was becoming too entangled in world affairs for its own good, going

President Woodrow Wilson toured the country in an effort to generate support for his peace plan after World War I.

against a tradition that dated back to George Washington's presidency. There was some stubbornness on both sides of the argument. Wilson tried to rally the nation to his side through a series of speeches but had a stroke during the tour. America was essentially without a leader until 1921. The Senate voted against ratifying the peace treaty, with its League of Nations. Without American participation, the

League was weak and ineffective during its relatively short period of existence.

The feeling that America should return to isolationism affected other parts of life, and here Communism starts to play a large role in our story. Businesses had boomed during World War I because of war-related production of goods. Interestingly, with so many men fighting overseas, women had to perform many of the factory jobs back home—which played a part in women earning the right to vote a few years later. With the war over, those soldiers returned home, only to see the economy shrink. There were few jobs for them.

Meanwhile, people had resumed immigrating to the United States. Some of the newcomers came from Eastern Europe, where Communism had established some roots. Longtime residents of the United States wondered why new immigrants were hired for jobs while they remained unemployed. And if those newcomers to America were hired, chances were good that they landed jobs that featured low pay and little job security. That made them perfect targets for union recruitment efforts.

Unions had been fighting for better wages, benefits, and working conditions since the end of the Civil War and through the rise of the **Technological Revolution** near the end of the nineteenth century. During World War I, President Wilson said unions were acting unpatriotically by asking for wage increases during a national emergency, and he asked for a wage freeze. Even though profits were large, the unions agreed to wait for raises.

However, when the war was over, the economic good times were over. The world economy, which had featured huge increases in international trade before 1914, had been torn apart by the war and its aftereffects. The cost of living in the United States, which had been contained during the war, was spiraling upward. The business owners claimed they didn't have the money for wage increases now. Besides, talk of workers uniting to take over companies, as they had done in Russia, was frightening to business leaders. In addition, those super-patriotic feelings of World War I didn't suddenly disappear from America on Armistice Day. Immigrants, Communists, and union members were considered particularly suspicious.

Mix it all together, and a "Red Scare" arrived. In hindsight, it all happened with astonishing speed—it arrived quickly and departed almost as fast.

Two of the major organizations of the time that came under fire were the Industrial Workers of the World, shortened to the IWW or the Wobblies, and the Socialist Party. The IWW was founded in 1905—the same year as Lenin's failed revolution in Russia—and it hoped to have all workers band together under one big tent. Membership went as high as 150,000 during World War I. Both the IWW and the Socialist Party were against American participation in World War I. Eugene Debs—one of the founders of the IWW and a presidential candidate for the Socialists in several elections— was arrested in 1918 for violating the Sedition Act. That law stated that criticizing the American war effort was against the law and would be subject to punishment. With the unions having some connections to Socialism, it didn't take much of a leap of imagination to believe that Communists were taking a greater role in the labor movement.

Strike in Seattle

The first major post-war strike came in January 1919. It took place in Seattle, as thirty-five thousand shipyard workers walked off their jobs. About two weeks later, a general strike was called for the city, and a total of sixty thousand people stopped reporting for work. Newspapers across the country followed the news of the job action, and the strikers themselves picked up the nickname of "reds," the color of the new flag of Russia.

Seattle mayor Ole Hansen, no friend of the IWW, announced that he would use police and federal troops to

A general strike in Seattle affected sixty thousand workers and received national attention.

break the strike. The general strike was called off after only four days. Hansen took the credit for the settlement, quit his job, and started a new career as a spokesman for anti-Communism. Strikes during the next few months were called "conspiracies against the government" and "plots to establish Communism" by the nation's newspapers.

May 1 was, at that point, a traditional day for labor activities around the world. The concept actually started in the United States. On May 1, 1886, rallies were staged in several cities in support of the eight-hour workday. The demonstrations continued through the next few days. On May 4, the rally in Chicago turned violent when a bomb went off and eleven people were killed. Eight people were arrested, tried, and convicted. The incident became known as the Haymarket Affair, and workers around the world subsequently started to mark the occasion with rallies on May 1. The tradition never caught on in America, but union rallies did take place in the United States on May 1, 1919. Riots broke out in New York, Boston, and other cities.

Tensions related to organized labor and immigrants were very present, then, when the American Legion was organized in St. Louis, Missouri, later that month. It was designed as an organization to improve morale among US veterans, but some of its members took it in an unexpected direction. Its constitution began this way:

> For God and Country we associate ourselves together for the following purposes: To uphold and defend the Constitution of the United States of America; to maintain

law and order; to foster and perpetuate a 100-percent Americanism; to preserve the memories and incidents of our association in the Great War [World War I]; to inculcate a sense of individual obligation to the community, state, and nation; to combat the autocracy of both the classes and the masses; to make right the master of might; to promote peace and good will on earth; to safeguard and transmit to posterity the principles of justice, freedom, and democracy; to consecrate and sanctify our comradeship by our devotion to mutual helpfulness.

The organization grew to one million members by the end of 1919—as opposed to the fifty thousand or so members of the Communist Party—and some of the Legionnaires took part in violent actions against perceived anti-Americans. The phrase "Leave the Reds to the Legion" grew in popularity.

Union members weren't the only targets for those who were afraid of so-called radicals. For example, teachers of higher education came under scrutiny for possibly having Communist viewpoints. That sort of scrutiny soon extended down to high schools, where many teachers were fired for membership in even the mildest of left-wing organizations— past or present. This "patriotic frenzy" eventually extended into government, and the public certainly had a legitimate reason to worry. Take yourself back in time to June 2, 1919, and considered how you might have reacted to the news of that particular day.

Anarchists Bomb Seven Cities

Luigi Galleani was an **anarchist**; he believed the United States should have no laws or government. Galleani was an extremist who believed he should use violent methods to further his cause. We'd call him a terrorist today. On that June night in 1919, bombs went off in seven American cities—Boston, Cleveland, New York, Paterson (New Jersey), Philadelphia, Pittsburgh, and Washington, DC—within a ninety-minute span. It's unclear if Galleani directed the bombings or if he simply inspired them among his followers.

Of those bombings, the most interesting story centers around the one in Washington, DC. Carlo Valdinoci—an editor of an anarchist publication—walked up to the front door of a house belonging to A. Mitchell Palmer, the attorney general of the United States, while carrying a bomb. The explosive device went off early. Not only did the bomb blow up the front of Palmer's house, but it killed Valdinoci. Palmer was not harmed.

All of the bombs had prominent targets such as businessmen, justice officials, and newspaper editors, and they had a piece of paper attached to the outside. Under the title "Plain Words," it read: "War, Class war, and you were the first to wage it under the cover of the powerful institutions you call order, in the darkness of your laws. There will have to be bloodshed; we will not dodge; there will have to be murder: we will kill, because it is necessary; there will have to be destruction; we will destroy to rid the world of your tyrannical institutions." Galleani was **deported** to his native Italy within three weeks of the bombings.

Radical Decision

There was plenty of discrimination and anger on display against radicals after the end of World War I. What may set the United States apart from other countries in this area is that bloodshed was at a minimum here. There were only two people who were executed in the period, and even their guilt remains an unsolved question almost one hundred years later.

Nicola Sacco, a shoemaker, and Bartolomeo Vanzetti, a fish peddler, were the people involved. On April 15, 1920, two men carrying a factory payroll of $15,776 were shot to death during a robbery in Braintree, Massachusetts, which

Nicola Sacco and Bartolomeo Vanzetti were executed for their alleged role in a pair of murders.

is located south of Boston. Sacco and Vanzetti were arrested three weeks later.

The two men were followers of Luigi Galleani, a radical anarchist, and both supported the violent overthrow of capitalism. Police linked Sacco's gun to the murders, although the connection may have been weak. Even so, the pair were convicted in a 1921 case that had testimony filled with prejudice against immigrants and so-called radicals.

Sacco and Vanzetti were electrocuted in 1927. Just before his death, Vanzetti said, "I wish to tell you I am innocent and never connected with any crime ... I wish to forgive some people for what they are now doing to me."

Several historians believe Sacco was guilty and Vanzetti was innocent. The scholars add that the evidence was not substantial enough to justify a conviction.

In 1977, Governor Michael Dukakis of Massachusetts signed a proclamation that said the pair had been treated unjustly.

That was merely the first step in the government's reactions to the bombings. For those who have studied America's reaction to the terrorist attacks in 2001, when the federal government created the Department of Homeland Security, the United States took a similar step in 1919. Many Americans sought a strong response to the bombings, and Palmer—perhaps thinking about a possible bid to become President in 1920—was ready. He created a General Intelligence Division inside of the Department of Justice. Palmer picked a bright young man to head the organization.

J. Edgar Hoover received his law degree in 1917 at the age of twenty-two. From there he took a job in the Justice Department and rose quickly to become the leader of the new Alien Enemy Bureau during World War I. President Wilson wanted that organization to find, arrest, and imprison disloyal foreigners without a trial. The bureau tracked down 1,400 "suspicious" Germans in the United States, arresting 98. When the war ended, Hoover became an obvious choice to lead the General Intelligence Division, since the functions of the two agencies were so similar.

Hoover's first step was to start a filing system. The General Intelligence Division started to collect information on organizations and individuals suspected to be radicals. It didn't take long to compile two hundred thousand filing cards. That led to the arrest of thousands of people who were said to be considered extremists; some were eventually deported. One person is said to have been arrested simply for looking like a radical.

As that effort continued, labor strikes were still considered by many to be anti-American and perhaps Communist inspired. On September 9, 1919, the Boston police force went on strike. A certain degree of panic set in, as the newspapers of the day pushed the belief that Bolsheviks were behind the walkout. On September 13, the entire police force was essentially fired, ending the strike. A steel strike began later that month that lasted until January 1920. It ended without the workers winning a single demand.

Hoover told Palmer that the radicals represented a threat to America, and the Justice Department's forces swung into action. On November 7, 1919, the second anniversary of the Bolshevik Revolution, agents conducted a raid on the Union of Russian Workers in New York City, using legislation passed during World War I as justification. Within a month, 249 radicals were placed on a ship and sent to Russia.

Roundup of Reds

The biggest show of force was yet to come. On January 2, 1920, government agents launched a series of raids in more than two dozen cities across the country. No one is even sure how many people were arrested that day, but estimates were in the thousands. Arrests outnumbered **warrants**, and some people were picked up by police simply for having a

J. Edgar Hoover spent much of his long career, most of it as the head of the Federal Bureau of Investigation, fighting Communism for the federal government.

foreign accent. In Hartford, anyone who even visited a friend who was in jail from the January 2 arrests was put in a cell. The massive raids represent the most famous moment of the first Red Scare. The era had other incidents of questionable actions by government officials. For example, it became illegal in thirty-two states simply to wave Communism's red flag.

A few months into 1920, it appeared that America's hostility toward foreigners had peaked. Maybe it was because some thought events had gone too far, and maybe it was because the movement against Communism just ran out of energy.

In the spring of 1920, several well-known attorneys attacked the Justice Department's actions that violated **civil liberties**. The expulsion of five Socialists from the New York State Assembly solely for their political views drew criticism from such people as Senator Warren Harding, a future President, and—surprisingly—Attorney General Palmer. Business leaders started to realize what might happen if immigrants were sent back to their homeland and thus taken out of the labor pool. Wages almost certainly would go up, and profits would go down.

The last major development in the era came on May 1, 1920. Palmer, having been told by investigators that radical forces were planning to overthrow the United States government on that date, predicted a revolution. Maybe a few of them were, but doing so is a tall order. When May 1 came and went without incident, Palmer was discredited. The attorney general's hopes of becoming president were finished.

The first Red Scare was over. While Communism presented a threat to America in those post-war years, the strong reaction had been out of proportion to the size of that threat. Communists were still living in the United States at that point, but the previous eighteen months hadn't done their public image much good. They essentially were driven out of sight. Such groups also had internal fights that frequently left them ineffective. Some of the radical leaders were still involved in the labor unions of the time, but their ideas didn't carry much weight.

Meanwhile, in Russia (which changed its name to the Soviet Union in 1922), changes were taking place. Lenin suffered a stroke in 1922, and moved into semi-retirement. Two men started positioning themselves as replacements for Lenin: Leon Trotsky and Joseph Stalin. Lenin and Stalin plotted political strategy together and became close. However, they reportedly had a falling out when Stalin insulted Lenin's wife. Lenin is said to have left orders that Stalin was not to take over the leadership role in government after his death.

Before those orders became widely known, though, Lenin suffered a bad heart attack in 1923. Stalin promptly started to work his way into a position of sole authority. When Lenin died, Stalin was ready. He won the struggle for power with Trotsky, whose supporters were given less important jobs in the Soviet government. As for Trotsky, he eventually was forced to leave the country. He was assassinated in Mexico under orders from Stalin in 1940.

Stalin Steps In

One of Stalin's first steps was to suggest that the Soviet Union essentially stop worrying about exporting Communist ideas to other countries, and start worrying about consolidating its gains and improving life in the areas it controlled. It was a popular move in the Soviet Union, as the people saw their nation fall further and further behind other countries economically as the recovery from World War I continued. Stalin's action meant the United States would be off the Soviet radar screen, making Communism less of a threat to America.

With Stalin more worried about current Communist nations than expanding Communism elsewhere, America's Communists were left in something of a state of confusion, and party membership in the United States shrank quickly. It could be argued that the Communists were thus unprepared to take advantage of a situation that developed in 1929.

World War I had left Europe in ruins, and it would take years to rebuild the economy there. In addition, the class system that had been in force in Europe for decades was damaged by the war. That led to more upheaval. It took until 1925 or so for European industry to rebound to pre–World War I levels, but it was still well behind the output of other countries.

After some initial difficulties with the transition from a war economy to a peacetime economy, America enjoyed large amounts of prosperity throughout the 1920s. Companies enjoyed record profits, which they invested into expansion of their business. Stock prices soared, and times were good for many.

But that sort of level of prosperity can't go on indefinitely. Eventually, some businesses fail, people are put out of work, goods go unpurchased, and economic activity decreases. Multiply that over several industries and a recession—a time when the economy as a whole in a nation shrinks—can take place. Today, government has some financial weapons to fight such situations, but in the 1920s, such a strategy ran counter to the political philosophy of the times.

Some observers could see some cracks in the economy before the autumn of 1929. These cracks became obvious to everyone in October of that year when the stock market crashed. The size of the losses resembled a snowball rolling down a huge hill, picking up size along the way until it overwhelmed everything in its path. Those who invested in the stock market suffered huge losses, and many of them were in no position to take on additional debt. Banks had no guarantees in place during times of panic, and some had large troubles when people started to withdraw their savings at a furious pace.

Great Depression Goes Global

The Great Depression of the 1930s is considered to be the worst in American history, even if economic numbers did improve slightly in the middle of that decade. What's more, the financial crash in America had a ripple effect. The United States had been an economic superpower in the 1920s. The crash caused spending to drop and then factories to close. European exports and banks worldwide were affected. The depression quickly spread around the world.

Karl Marx had predicted that the capitalist nations would more or less "blow up," and to some it looked as if this was starting to come true. Therefore, this could have been a very fertile time for recruitment by Communist groups. It wasn't, for reasons that will be explored here shortly, but gains were made. Membership in the Communist Party of the United States reached seventy-five thousand in the late 1930s.

The Communist Party of the United States always thought of the working class as its natural ally, and it would figure that it would first seek out those who had the least to lose in trying to gain members. There was little question that African Americans of that time fit that description. Many blacks in

The case of the Scottsboro Boys drew wide attention in the 1930s.

the South were still trying to survive by **sharecropping** on farms. They had no political power at all, since most had lost the right to vote about fifty years before the Depression arrived. Those who had fled the South for the North weren't much better off. Those blacks often lived in poverty as well and were victims of discrimination.

In addition, a world Communist group had voted to order the American branch of the organization to recruit African Americans. In order to accomplish that goal, the Communist Party had to fully integrate, which meant not only were blacks allowed to hold positions of authority, but the party had to take an official position of supporting interracial marriage. It's certainly possible, considering that such marriages were not accepted by much of society in that era, that the stance may have hurt the organization's popularity.

The most famous case of the Communists supplying aid to blacks came early in the 1930s. It came to be known as the Scottsboro Boys matter. Nine young African Americans between the ages of thirteen and twenty-one were accused of raping two white women on a train in Alabama. The evidence was not convincing, but the nine were quickly convicted anyway, and all but one were sentenced to death.

The International Labor Defense, part of the Communist Party, jumped in to help the nine young men with their cases. One of the defendants denied that she was raped in January 1932, but that did not matter to the Alabama Supreme Court. It voted, 6–1, to uphold all but one of the death sentences. The eighth death sentence was reversed on the grounds that the young man was a juvenile.

The case was then heard by the United States Supreme Court, and its decision certainly surprised some. The court voted, 7–2, to overturn the lower court's ruling. The reasoning was that the blacks did not have adequate representation in their first trial, a violation of the Fourteenth Amendment to the Constitution, which guaranteed **due process**. It was a major legal milestone for blacks in this country.

The story became much more complicated from that point, as legal actions went on through the next decade. Many of the young men were tried again and in some cases convicted again, while charges against others were dropped. Some of them served time in prison, but none were executed.

Clarence Norris was the last of the Scottsboro Boys to die, passing away in 1989. He had been sentenced to death in 1938, but that was changed to life in prison later that year. Norris was paroled in 1946 and pardoned by Governor George Wallace in 1976. The last chapter was written in 2013, when Governor Robert Bentley pardoned all nine of the Scottsboro Boys.

Even with those efforts, the Communist Party never established a strong presence among African Americans. One reason was that many blacks preferred to stick together in their fight for civil rights. Another was that Communism still carried a stigma in the United States, which was left over from the original "Red Scare" days.

But two other developments played a big role as to why people didn't join the Communist Party in large numbers. Franklin D. Roosevelt was elected president in 1932, and within days of taking office in 1933, he took immediate action to battle the depression. It was a more liberal, activist program than his predecessors had used, and unions experienced a period of growth. In addition, Roosevelt immediately ordered that the United States give diplomatic recognition to the Soviet Union, allowing the two governments to formally speak to each other after sixteen years of silence.

In addition, Adolf Hitler took over as chancellor of Germany in 1933. His political philosophy was called Fascism, a right-wing dictatorship with strong elements of nationalism. Less than twenty years after its total defeat in World War I, Germany started to show signs of becoming an aggressive world power again. Communists were worried about what that might mean for the Soviet Union and the world, and opted to spend much of their small political capital on fighting Fascism.

Their fears, and the fears of the rest of the world, turned out to be justified. The complicated relationship between the United States and its Communist citizens was about to take some dramatic turns.

TWO

Friends and Enemies

I t wasn't easy to be a member of the Communist Party of the United States in the late 1930s and the 1940s. The group's basic beliefs had to change whenever there was a shift in global politics—and there were some dramatic realignments during that era.

The discussion starts with Germany in the 1930s. Adolf Hitler took control of the government in 1933 and slowly accumulated power. In 1934, he ordered internal security forces to break up any rival organizations that might threaten his base of power. In 1935, he put into effect the Nuremburg Laws that essentially made discrimination against Jews the law of the land.

The steps came more rapidly after that. Hitler broke the Treaty of Versailles that ended World War I by creating a military force for Germany. England and France probably could have stopped Germany from rearming, but neither country was willing to do so. The events of World War I

Opposite: Soviet foreign minister Viacheslav Molotov signs a nonaggression pact with Germany.

were so horrible and so memorable that neither victorious country wanted to start on the road to a repeat. The military buildup went so effortlessly for Germany that Hitler became even more ambitious.

In 1938, German troops marched into Austria and occupied that nation, another violation of the Treaty of Versailles. Later that year, Hitler demanded that part of Czechoslovakia, the Sudetenland, be awarded to Germany. In a meeting with leaders of England and France, Germany was allowed to take the Sudetenland if that would satisfy Hitler. He said it would, and German troops marched into the region without firing a shot, while Czech authorities had no say in the fate of part of their country. British prime minister Neville Chamberlain famously flew home after agreeing to a treaty with Germany, saying that the document promised "peace in our time."

The entire world was watching the situation, and that included the Communist Party in the United States. That group's anti-Fascist beliefs won them some support from non-Communists. The Communist Party also supported some programs and projects that were part of Franklin Roosevelt's New Deal. It worked to form unions that would join the Congress of Industrial Organizations (CIO).

Hitler Moves Quickly

Events deteriorated quickly in 1939. Germany took over the rest of Czechoslovakia in March. At that point, England and France finally realized that Hitler would continue to try to expand Germany's domination throughout Europe. They belatedly drew a proverbial line in the sand. If Germany attacked a free Poland, there would be war.

That led to a diplomatic treaty in August 1939 that caught almost the entire world, including Communists in the United States, by complete surprise. Germany and the Soviet Union signed a nonaggression pact, which split Eastern Europe into two areas—one under German control and one under Soviet control. With England and France unwilling to stop the Germans, the Soviets were afraid that the Germans would set their sights to the east and continue to march toward their territory. For Germany, it was the final step before an invasion of Poland could take place.

On September 1, 1939, that German invasion happened. About two weeks later, the Soviets attacked Poland from the east. World War II had begun.

We can only imagine what sort of reaction this had among Communists in the US. Their comrades in the Soviet Union had been critical of Nazi Germany for almost six years. Now the USSR and Germany were allies. The Communist Party's official positions on the world situation had to change quickly, no matter how hypocritical it might seem.

The Communist Party line on the world situation became that England and France had started an imperialist war, all evidence to the contrary. Unions that had strong ties to the Communists frequently went out on strike. While the Germans and Soviets were busy recording military successes in Europe, America was doing what it could to help the forces of Britain and France without sending troops to the conflict. The Communist Party labeled that as "war-mongering."

By 1940, the forces of the Soviet Union and Germany were on the march. The Soviets grabbed the small Baltic nations of Lithuania, Latvia, and Estonia, and made them part of their own nation. They also attacked Finland. Germany, meanwhile, looked west—having signed a treaty with the only country that could be a problem in the east. It attacked France and quickly occupied it. England was alone in Europe as a democratic nation. British prime minister Winston Churchill turned to the United States for aid, and President Roosevelt provided as much of it as he legally could without declaring war.

The 1940 United States presidential elections went on as scheduled, and the Communist Party fielded a candidate: Earl Browder. It's interesting to note that the party was allowed to

Communist Party leader Earl Browder campaigned for president in 1940.

be placed on ballots, but Browder himself was not allowed to travel during the election period, and he could only issue recorded and written campaign statements.

After a failed attempt to break Great Britain's will through the use of air strikes, Hitler pondered his next move. Most of Europe was either under his control or run by allies such as Italy and the Soviet Union. His armies seemed almost invincible. What would he do next?

The answer was one more giant surprise, especially to the Communist Party of the United States. Hitler attacked the Soviet Union.

The Nazis had expressed a desire to take over Soviet territory for German settlement since they began to organize in the 1920s. Hitler had never thought that the nonaggression treaty with the Soviets was anything but a tactical maneuver. Once Western Europe was relatively secure, he decided in December 1940 to plan an attack on the Soviet Union. "Operation Barbarossa" began on June 22, 1941.

When the Soviets switched sides in World War II, the Communists did the same. It was a dizzying time in history, proof of the age-old saying in diplomacy: "The enemy of my enemy is my friend." Suddenly the war effort was no longer "imperialist," it was "democratic."

The stakes grew even larger on December 7, 1941, when the Japanese attacked Pearl Harbor in Hawaii. In one of the great mysteries of World War II, Hitler's Germany declared war on the United States a few days later. Even though Japan and Germany were allies, the Germans were under no obligation under the terms of their treaty with Japan to fight the Americans. Hitler did it anyway. Thus, he added a potentially powerful new enemy in what figured to be a long global conflict. America had not been touched by the war's effects for the most part, and needed only time to train large numbers of soldiers and build enormous amounts of military hardware such as planes and tanks.

Thus, the United States, Soviet Union and Great Britain all joined together for the long and painstaking process of destroying the German war machine. The English, who at one point were standing almost alone in the fight against the Germans, now had two powerful partners. The catch was that the Americans and Soviets didn't trust each other but had to coexist in order to gain victory.

Communists Back Off

Back in America, the Communists changed their positions and rhetoric completely. Any antiwar materials issued by the party headed for the nearest wastebasket. Strikes by unions were discouraged for the length of the war. The name of the party was even changed in 1944, when it was known as the "Communist Political Organization."

It's not necessary to review World War II in much detail here. Germany forgot its world history and soon learned how difficult it is to attack Soviet territory in winter, as the war on the so-called eastern front quickly bogged down. American and British forces invaded France on June 6, 1944, taking some of the pressure off Soviet forces. Attacks by two mighty armies from opposite directions made a German defeat almost inevitable.

Those mighty armies had another effect as well. At the Yalta Conference in early 1945, Roosevelt, Stalin, and Churchill formally agreed to what already was practically true. Europe was to be divided into spheres of influence— with countries taking the lead role in the postwar world of specific areas.

Winston Churchill, Franklin Roosevelt, and Joseph Stalin met at the Yalta Conference in 1945 to discuss the postwar world.

Germany surrendered in April 1945, but the postwar maneuvering was already in full flight. Soviet forces controlled most of Eastern Europe, giving Stalin the outcome in the war that he sought. An incident from the Potsdam Conference in the summer of 1945 tells much about the relationship between the United States and the Soviet Union. US president Harry Truman, who had replaced Roosevelt after the latter died in April, met with Churchill and Stalin to discuss the end of the war with Japan as well as postwar matters in Europe. Truman told Stalin that the United States had developed an atomic bomb that it would use on Japan in the very near future. Truman expected some level of surprise from Stalin, but the Soviet leader had no reaction. He already had been told about the bomb by his spies in America.

The Soviet Union—and before that, Russia—always had been insecure, partly because of the frequent invasions by world powers that had killed millions of its people, and partly because it was usually a step behind the Western nations in modernization and machinery. The Soviets also carried some fears during World War II that the next target for American atomic bombs might be the USSR. That drove them to place spies in such key places as the atomic research areas in New Mexico during World War II, and to start to develop a nuclear device of their own as soon as possible. The atomic bomb was used for the first time as a weapon of mass destruction about a month later. The United States dropped one on both Hiroshima and Nagasaki, bringing an end to the conflict with Japan.

With the fighting in Europe and Asia now over, it was time to assemble the pieces created by World War II. The Soviet Union saw this period as a chance to expand its influence as well as create a "**buffer zone**" to help prevent future attacks by foreign armies. The USSR started to take steps to solidify its control of captured territory in Eastern Europe.

Back in the United States, some of the conditions that existed at the end of World War I had returned less than thirty years later. The United States had crossed oceans to end tyranny, and its people were anxious to pack up and go home. But now there was another threat that seemed to be building in that part of the world, featuring a dictator in Stalin who sounded about as ruthless as the one who led Nazi Germany.

After the war, most of the world's Communist parties — following orders from Moscow — ended their passive stances toward democracy and started to return to their original political positions. That included the Communist Party of the United States. The transition was a little quick for some of its leaders, who left the party rather than return to the role of adversary of the United States government.

A power vacuum existed in the world, with most of the great countries recovering from the war's aftereffects. England, for example, had gone from the world's greatest creditor nation to the world's greatest debtor nation during the course of World War II. The United States had to fill that space. The Truman administration realized that this was not the time for isolationism, and that vigilance against a growing Communist threat was necessary. The American government needed to convince its citizens of the need to stand up to the menace represented by the Soviet Union and its supporters.

There was a drawback to that strategy. It would generate a great deal of fear of the Communists, and that would lead to internal abuses of civil liberties and the rise of opportunists who could use the situation for their own political gain. In other words, another "Red Scare" was about to begin.

It didn't take long for the Soviet Union to start causing problems in the postwar world. The three major nations had agreed to start removing their forces from Iraq early in 1946. The Americans and British exited as scheduled, but the Soviets didn't appear to be going anywhere. And in February of that year, Stalin told an audience in Moscow that Communism and capitalism could not coexist.

In March 1946, only three days after the Soviet Union missed its deadline for leaving Iraq, a British visitor to the United States gave one of the most famous speeches in that period of history. It came at a relatively unlikely place: Westminster College in Fulton, Missouri.

Churchill Charts a Course

Winston Churchill had been voted out of office as Great Britain's Prime Minister shortly after the end of the war, much to the surprise of a watching world. President Truman invited him to the United States, and he took the opportunity to give a major speech on his trip. About forty thousand people—more than seven times the population of Fulton—were there to hear it. Churchill offered a chilling commentary on the events taking place at that time:

Winston Churchill's "Iron Curtain" speech marked the moment when the Soviet Union became an adversary of the United States and Great Britain.

From Stettin in the Baltic to Trieste in the Adriatic, an iron curtain has descended across the Continent. Behind that line lie all the capitals of the ancient states of Central and Eastern Europe. Warsaw, Berlin, Prague, Vienna, Budapest, Belgrade, Bucharest, and Sofia, all these famous cities and the populations around them lie in what I must call the Soviet sphere, and all are subject, in one form or another, not only to Soviet influence but to a very high and, in many cases, increasing measure of control from Moscow.

Athens alone—Greece with its immortal glories—is free to decide its future at an election under British, American, and French observation. The Russian-dominated Polish Government has been encouraged to make enormous and wrongful inroads upon Germany, and mass expulsions of millions of Germans on a scale grievous and undreamed-of are now taking place. The Communist parties, which were very small in all these Eastern States of Europe, have been raised to preeminence and power far beyond their numbers and are seeking everywhere to obtain totalitarian control. Police governments are prevailing in nearly every case, and so far, except in Czechoslovakia, there is no true democracy.

For those in the audience who were nervous about rising Communist influence, Churchill's "Iron Curtain" speech gave Americans even more reasons to worry. It completely changed the conversation about the Soviet Union, turning an important ally into a threat to democratic nations around the world.

Tensions continued to grow as 1946 moved along. In July, the United States tested an atomic bomb on a tiny island in the Pacific Ocean called Bikini Atoll. Yes, the two-piece bathing suit was named after the area after the test received large amounts of publicity, but an atomic explosion was serious business—the first since World War II.

Truman Doctrine

In Europe, Communists were active in the European nations along the Mediterranean Sea as the postwar rebuilding program continued. It was no surprise, then, when the so-called Truman Doctrine was announced. When President Truman asked Congress for $400 million in aid to Turkey and Greece, he issued a sweeping statement about such actions. The government's policy would be "to support free peoples who are resisting attempted subjugation by armed minorities or by outside pressures."

That eventually led to the Marshall Plan, a massive relief program engineered by General George Marshall, who was

President Harry Truman signs the Economic Assistance Act, authorizing the Marshall Plan that extended aid to defeated nations and to Eastern Europe.

serving as secretary of state. In a speech in June 1947, Marshall said the United States "should do whatever it is able to do to assist in the return of normal economic health to the world, without which there can be no political stability and no assured peace." It was an unprecedented act of generosity— never before had a victorious nation in war offered to help rebuild the defeated side on such a scale. The offer of aid even extended to the Soviet Union and the Eastern European nations it controlled, but it was turned down.

Even so, the American position that was implied in the Truman Doctrine was specific. If the Soviet Union tried to extend its influence to new nations, the United States would try to stop it. The friendship of World War II was officially over. This was a whole new era. It also meant that this was no time for an American to have Communist beliefs or sympathies.

Who suffered the most during the next several years? Much of the weight of the situation fell on three groups in particular: government workers, unions, and entertainers. The year 1947 was a particularly bad one for all three.

Only days after the announcement of the Truman Doctrine, President Truman signed an executive order called the Loyalty-Security Program. Charges by conservative politicians had been made that Communists were working for the federal government and that Truman wasn't "tough enough" to keep them out. Such charges had played a key role in the Congressional elections of 1946, as Republicans took control of both houses of Congress for the first time since 1932. This action from the White House was the response. Federal employees had to sign a pledge stating that they had "complete and unswerving loyalty" to the United States of America.

Spies certainly worked in the federal government, so some of the fears were justified. Enforcement was the obvious problem. After all, anyone with Communist views could sign a form without meaning it. Therefore, loyalty boards were set up in the various departments of government. The Federal Bureau of Investigation checked into the backgrounds of employees. If there were reasonable doubts of someone's views, that person could lose his or her job. A loyalty review board handled appeals.

That, in turn, raised the question of how someone with subversive views might be identified. After all, few people at that scary time were willing to go public about Communist or Socialist viewpoints. One way was to start up a list of "suspicious groups." It became known as the "Attorney General's List of Subversive Organizations" or AGLOSO. A similar list had been drawn up by the Roosevelt administration starting in 1941; it contained about a dozen names of organizations but no individuals. After Truman's loyalty order, the number went up greatly.

Such a system had some serious drawbacks. It was difficult to determine exactly what groups could be considered subversive. That's because the guidelines about placement on the list were so vague. Those doing the investigating had unlimited investigative power, and thus were above the law.

At first, government officials did not even reveal what groups were on AGLOSO. If information cast suspicion on a group, the organization and all of its members would be considered security risks. The groups on the list finally were released in December 1947, but even then there were problems. What if you joined the organization without having knowledge that it had Communist tendencies? What if you joined a friend in attending one meeting, and thus had your name turn up on a membership list somewhere? You easily could lose your job or your career. The list also was used by a variety of other businesses, some with connections to government work. Therefore, AGLOSO had a potential impact on a wide range of people, and not only the sixty thousand or so who were estimated to be members of the Communist Party.

Investigators put a lot of work into this effort, checking out some 4.5 million people over a ten-year period. About 5,000 people reportedly left their jobs before their individual investigations took place. It's impossible to know how many of those people were actually Communists, how many at least leaned that way politically, and how many simply objected to the idea of an investigation for one reason or another. Meanwhile, 378 either lost their jobs or were turned down in their request to be hired for one.

In hindsight, it's easy to wonder if anyone had thought much about the legalities of such actions. But this tense time quieted many of those who wondered about whether the AGLOSO list was a violation of our civil liberties. People worried about civil liberties were badly outnumbered. Conservatives tended to like the idea of the list, while liberals argued about how such investigations would take place rather than talk about whether the entire idea was a proper and legal one.

Supreme Court Hears Cases

A couple of cases did reach the Supreme Court a few years later, but the judicial rulings were rather confusing. In one case, the court ruled that a woman still had the right to associate with anyone, but that the government had the right not to hire her. In a similar case, the court ruled that the attorney general had used poor methods for coming up with the list. The rulings had little effect on the political atmosphere.

A few months later, a second domino fell in the battle against Communist sympathizers. The bill in Congress was called the Labor-Management Relations Act of 1947, but everyone called it the Taft-Hartley Act, named after cosponsors Robert Taft of Ohio and Fred Hartley of New Jersey. It was a revision of the so-called Wagner Act, which was passed in the middle of the Roosevelt Administration in 1935 and deserves some explanation.

The Wagner Act was considered "labor's bill of rights." It covered most of those participating in interstate commerce and gave workers the right to join unions, to bargain collectively, and to go on strike. The National Labor Relations Board was created to administer the rules. But by 1947, the political landscape had changed because Republicans had taken control of Congress. Several freshmen representatives, including a California congressman by the name of Richard Nixon, were intent on rolling back some of the provisions of Roosevelt's New Deal. Eventually they succeeded in the area of labor relations. The Taft-Hartley Act added restrictions to labor's rights. President Truman vetoed the legislation, but

Congress passed the bill with more than a two-thirds majority to put it into effect.

Most of the portions of the law dealt with the rights of workers and hiring practices, and they did not apply to political ideologies. However, the act also required union officials to sign a document and swear to an oath that they were not Communists. Did they sign it? How much of a choice did they have? Many thought the law was a violation of their constitutional rights, but they obeyed it anyway. Consider the remarks of Leon Sverdlove of the Jewelry Workers of New York, who said union members who leaned toward the Communists made a slight adjustment in their thinking in order for their union careers to continue:

> We made the turn, and we became, what shall I say—more moderate. But that didn't prevent us from continuing to sponsor, to participate in anything that was progressive. I would say that the connection that was severed was one of a specific left-wing policy sponsored by the Communists at that time. That's what we broke with.

The third and final domino of 1947 fell in October when the House Un-American Activities Committee (HUAC) began hearings on the role of Communists in the entertainment industry.

HUAC had been around since 1938. Its initial task was to find Nazi sympathizers, but the scope of the committee's mission quickly expanded to include Communists as well. Supporters thought HUAC performed a vital role in national security, while detractors believed it was merely a way to attack President Roosevelt. No one denied that the hearings involved in such searches were dramatic and attracted attention.

After World War II, there was no need for HUAC to look for Nazis, so attention focused solely on Communists. The committee did spend time examining government and labor, but soon it looked at Hollywood as a major target for investigation. At first, this appeared to be a strange choice; liberal filmmakers and actors must have been less important than spies in our government. But the line of thought was that movies were watched by huge numbers of people each week, and Communists might try to use those productions as something of a tool for political purposes. Besides, the

Walt Disney was among the members of the entertainment industry who testified in front of the House Un-American Activities Committee in 1947.

popularity of films almost guaranteed a great deal of publicity for Congressional hearings into the industry.

It's fair to say that the employees in the entertainment business probably were—and continue to be—more liberal than the population as a whole. Some directors and artists had been a part of Communist organizations during the 1930s. What's more, some movies offered opinions with a slant to the liberal side of the political spectrum.

Sympathizers Identified

Before the hearings opened, HUAC had asked forty-one people connected with the entertainment industry to come to testify about their political beliefs. The names of many of those invited to testify came from an article in the *Hollywood Reporter* that listed entertainment employees with Communist connections. Those people who agreed to confess an association with the Communist Party gave the committee the names of fellow members. But some nineteen others refused to answer such questions. Out of that group, eleven declared themselves as "unfriendly witnesses." One of them, playwright Bertolt Brecht, testified falsely that he wasn't ever a Communist and moved to Communist East Berlin the next day.

The rest of the group soon became known as the Hollywood Ten: Alvah Bessie, Herbert Biberman, Lester Cole, Edward Dmytryk, Ring Lardner Jr., John Howard Lawson, Albert Maltz, Samuel Ornitz, Adrian Scott, and Dalton Trumbo. They refused to answer questions at public hearings, such as "Are you now or have you ever been a member of the Communist Party?" based on First Amendment protections.

Several of them also took the opportunity to verbally attack committee members. Lawson's testimony was so hostile that he was ejected from the session. All of the members of the Hollywood Ten received contempt of Congress charges.

HUAC eventually sentenced all ten to a year in prison and fined them $1,000 each. They also were fired by movie studio executives and could not find work in any area of the business. The so-called **blacklist** had begun. Dmytryk, a celebrated director, left the country for England in 1948, but eventually returned to the United States, where he was arrested and imprisoned. In prison, he decided he'd been fooled by the Communists. Dmytryk eventually returned to testify before HUAC in 1951, and he admitted that he had been a member of the Communist Party in 1944–45. He also supplied the names of twenty-six party members. Dmytryk was allowed to return to work in the entertainment industry after that. Among his most famous films was *The Caine Mutiny*.

World tensions continued to grow in the final two years of the 1940s. The Communists staged a coup in Czechoslovakia in February 1948, and took control of that country in brutal fashion. Any opposition to the Marshall Plan in Congress melted away, and it was signed into law in April of that year.

The presidential campaign offered a little relief to everyone in 1948. The Republican Party, still riding the wave from the 1946 Congressional elections, was counting on placing New York governor Thomas E. Dewey in the White House. The relatively primitive polling done at the time had Dewey winning easily. Therefore, it was a big surprise on election night when Truman actually won the election. The result guaranteed that American policies would not change drastically in the next four years.

During that campaign, Truman had to split his attention between political matters and world affairs, and one such development was particularly serious.

After World War II, Germany had been divided into four occupation areas, controlled by the United States, Great Britain, France, and the Soviet Union. Berlin, the German capital, was located roughly in the middle of the Soviet zone and also was split into four occupation zones. The American, British, and French zones were grouped in what was called West Berlin, which was completely surrounded by Soviet territory. On June 24, 1948, the Soviets stopped all traffic on roads and railways headed into West Berlin.

Planes carrying food and supplies streamed into Berlin for almost a year after the Soviets blockaded the German city.

The blockade left Berlin without access to food and other day-to-day supplies.

It was the biggest crisis in the **Cold War** to that point. Many believed World War III was about to start. Truman and his advisors came up with another plan, though. They would fly food and supplies into Berlin in a fleet of airplanes. The Allies had been guaranteed three flight routes into Berlin by the Soviets. The logistics were difficult—Berlin had two million people at the time—and it took time to gear up the relief efforts. After several months, the Soviets finally were convinced that the Western nations were not going to abandon Berlin. They lifted the blockade on May 12, 1949.

Any good feeling about a peaceful outcome in Berlin did not last long, as other events fed into the anti-Communist feelings still raging in the United States. On August 29, 1949, the Soviet Union exploded its first atomic bomb. America's monopoly on nuclear weapons was gone. Then, on October 1, 1949, the Communists declared victory in China's Civil War. Communist expansion had claimed its biggest prize to date, the most populous nation on earth. The question that came up throughout the United States after that was "Who lost China?"—as if it were America's to lose.

The end of the decade was a nervous time in America under the circumstances. What was missing was a person who could become a focal point for the anti-Communist feelings and actions that were taking place in the nation.

There was someone ready and willing to take that role, and he would etch his name in the American history books.

THREE

Tailgunner Joe

The date was February 9, 1950, and the place was Wheeling, West Virginia. A group of Republican women filed into the McClure Motel. The Ohio County Women's Republican Club was staging a banquet to celebrate Lincoln's Birthday, and they had convinced a senator to come to Wheeling to address the group. It was unusual for a senator from Wisconsin to show up in Wheeling, a place not known for its impact on national political events. However, politicians have given speeches like this for years, without creating any stir. By all accounts, this particular senator enjoyed such functions, and apparently was pretty good at giving speeches.

Most politicians give predictable speeches at events like this one, so the ladies of Wheeling would not have been prepared for what was spoken by Senator Joseph McCarthy. What they heard was a speech that had a huge impact on American history. Before we get to that speech, let's look at the times in which it was set. Of particular importance was a well-publicized legal case that had been just decided.

Opposite: **The testimony of Whittaker Chambers was a springboard for the rise of Joe McCarthy.**

The story of Whittaker Chambers and Alger Hiss is an odd one. Chambers had joined the Communist Party around 1925. He became a spy for that organization, and claimed that in the 1930s he worked with a Communist group in Washington that included several members of the Roosevelt administration. However, Chambers soon became dissatisfied by the policies of the Soviet Union, and left the Communist Party in 1938. He became more upset with the Communists when the Soviets signed a nonaggression pact with Germany in 1939. Chambers gave to the federal government the names of several people who he claimed had worked with Communists. The FBI looked into it, but it was more concerned with Nazi Germany at that point in history.

Chambers started to work for *Time* magazine in 1939, and he was still there as a writer and editor when he spoke at a hearing by the House Un-American Activities Committee in 1948. Chambers gave several names of alleged Communists to the committee. Hiss was one of them.

Hiss had worked for the Roosevelt administration in a variety of roles. He left government service in 1946, taking a job with the Carnegie Endowment for International Peace. That organization tries to promote international cooperation and understanding. Hiss's career came to an abrupt halt when Chambers made the charge on August 3, 1948, that Hiss was a member of the Communist Party. Hiss had his turn two days later. He testified before HUAC that the accusation was untrue. He later filed a defamation suit against Chambers.

The House Committee had little enthusiasm for exploring the matter of who was telling the truth in the case but created a subcommittee to look into it. The chairman of that subcommittee was Richard Nixon, who had received information from the FBI that suggested a link between Hiss and the Communists.

On August 25, Chambers and Hiss both appeared before HUAC, and gave their sides of the story. It marked the first time in history that a Congressional hearing was televised. Chambers was confident and consistent in his testimony, enough to make Hiss something of a target of anti-Communist feelings that were growing among the public. Later that year, Chambers produced some documents that he said would back up his claim that Hiss was a Communist. Chambers had hidden some of them in a hollowed-out pumpkin and buried them; they became known as the "Pumpkin Papers."

Hiss eventually was charged with two counts of perjury. The initial trial ended in a hung jury, but in the retrial, Hiss was found guilty. A judge sentenced him to five years in jail in January 1950. Thus, a former member of the State Department had been convicted for lying about his status as a Communist.

Scientist Spy

In that same month, another development involving a Communist spy rattled the free world. Klaus Fuchs was born in Germany but left for England in 1933 when Hitler took power. He was a brilliant scientist who worked on the atomic bomb project in the United States during World War II.

In 1949, after returning to England, Fuchs was confronted by British intelligence officials who said he was mentioned in a Soviet coded message. He confessed in January 1950 to sending detailed information on the atomic bomb to the Soviets in 1945, and to sending other information about the hydrogen bomb to the USSR in 1946 and 1947. Fuchs's explanation was that he joined the Communists while living in Germany because he thought it was the only group that could stop the Nazis, and he remained loyal to that action. He soon would be convicted in England after a trial that lasted ninety minutes, and he was sentenced to fourteen years in prison. Along the way, it became obvious that the Soviets had several sources of information from people involved in the atomic bomb project during World War II. This added to the public's fears over Communism.

The Hiss decision and the Fuchs confession were fresh on everyone's minds when Senator McCarthy took to the lectern in Wheeling a couple of weeks later. Much of the audience was about to be introduced to him. All that most club members knew about him was that he was a senator.

Joseph McCarthy was born in Wisconsin in 1908. He graduated from law school in 1935 and was elected as a judge in 1937. McCarthy enlisted in the Marines during World War II. Even though his job through much of the war was to debrief returning pilots, McCarthy created a false image for himself upon returning. He became "Tailgunner Joe," who embellished the details of his military career by claiming he flew on missions to Japan several times.

McCarthy surprised incumbent Senator Robert La Follette Jr., a labor supporter, in the Republican primary of 1946. In the general election campaign, he charged opponent Howard McMurray with being willing to accept Communist

Joe McCarthy inflated his war record during his successful campaign for senator from Wisconsin in 1946.

aid in the political race. While no one was willing to accept the help of Communists at this point, the charge stuck, and McCarthy became a senator. He had little impact upon the Senate after taking office. One survey of reporters labeled him the worst senator in the country.

By 1950, McCarthy was best known for his work on such issues as ending the rationing of sugar. That led to an investigation for tax evasion and for taking bribes from the

Pepsi-Cola Company. The senator was three years through his six-year term in office, and he needed an issue to capture the imagination of the public as his reelection bid in 1952 closed in.

So the man who got up from his chair to give a speech at the McClure Hotel was ready to create a stir, although he didn't think it would happen on this particular day. Otherwise, McCarthy would have given the speech in a bigger place than Wheeling. He talked about a war between "two diametrically opposed ideologies," and that we were preparing for "a final, all-out battle between communistic atheism and Christianity." Then came a comment on how traitors to the American way of life were in our midst, and that led to this famous quotation:

> Ladies and gentlemen, while I cannot take the time to name all the men in the State Department who have been named as active members of the Communist Party and members of a spy ring, I have here in my hand a list of 205—a list of names that were made known to the Secretary of State as being members of the Communist Party and who nevertheless are still working and shaping policy in that State Department.

McCarthy went on to make references to the Hiss case and take questions from the audience on a variety of subjects. When he finished that speech, he was on his way to becoming the most famous anti-Communist in America.

Did he have such a list in his hand? It seems unlikely. A 1946 letter by Secretary of State James Byrnes implied that 205 members of the State Department were security risks. But

Kennedy Connection

Robert F. Kennedy and Joseph McCarthy seem like an odd combination at first glance. Kennedy became a national figure as a voice for those Americans who were rarely heard, while McCarthy tried to silence the voices of others.

Yet the two did work together in 1953 and 1954. McCarthy was a friend of Robert Kennedy's father, Joseph. They were both strong anti-Communists and shared Irish-Catholic roots. McCarthy visited the Kennedy compound at Hyannis Port, Massachusetts, and was the godfather for Robert Kennedy's first child.

Kennedy was the campaign manager for brother John in a 1952 Senate campaign. After the election, Robert worked with the Senate Subcommittee on Investigations, which was chaired by McCarthy. Kennedy's investigative work revealed that some of America's allies were selling goods to China during the Korean War. Kennedy soon grew tired of McCarthy's investigative tactics and those of McCarthy's aide, Roy Cohn. Kennedy resigned from his position.

A day after McCarthy was condemned by the Senate, Kennedy was on a boat with some reporters. "Why do you reporters ... feel the way you do?" he asked. "OK, Joe's methods may be a little rough, but after all, his goal was to expose Communists in government—a worthy goal. So why are you reporters so critical of his methods?"

Kennedy later returned to a position on that same subcommittee and helped to write a report criticizing McCarthy's behavior as the chairman of the subcommittee.

in reality, the number of those people still in their jobs had decreased, and they had passed additional security checks. What's more, McCarthy sent a telegram to President Truman two days later saying that the number of Communists in the State Department was 57. McCarthy demanded that Truman take immediate action. He also stated, "Failure on your part will label the Democratic Party of being the bedfellow of international Communism."

Author David Halberstam suggested McCarthy believed that some of those people weren't simply naïve, but had committed treason. China, taken over by Communists led by Mao Zedong in the 1949 revolution, couldn't have collapsed because of a corrupt and outdated political system, McCarthy reasoned. It had to be some sort of Soviet conspiracy. And, the Senator concluded, the Democrats were "soft" on Communism—a charge that was difficult to judge or prove, but one that affected foreign policy in this country for decades.

It did not take long for the Senate to react to McCarthy's actions. The Senate Foreign Relations Committee was ordered to investigate McCarthy's charge by creating a special subcommittee. The chairman of that group was Millard Tydings of Maryland. The hearings lasted from March to July of 1950, and the conversation was often loud and stormy.

McCarthy submitted the names of 110 people whom he wanted investigated, probably taken from a House investigation done a few years before. The Truman administration allowed the subcommittee to look at the loyalty files of seventy-one of those people, and nine of them were invited to testify. Six did so.

Declaration of Conscience

At that same time, a member of the Senate spoke on that legislative body's floor about McCarthy's charges. Senator Margaret Chase Smith of Maine delivered her "Declaration of Conscience" speech on June 1. After criticizing Democratic leadership, Senator Smith said, "The nation sorely needs a Republican victory. But I don't want to see the Republican Party ride to political victory on the Four Horsemen of **Calumny**— Fear, Ignorance, Bigotry, and Smear." McCarthy responded by calling Smith "Moscow Maggie."

The results of the investigation were issued in July, and voting strictly followed party lines. The majority report of the committee, approved by three Democrats including Tydings, cleared the witnesses. It stated that McCarthy's exaggerations were "a fraud and a hoax perpetrated on the Senate of the United States and the American people." One Republican, Senator William Jennings of Indiana, criticized Tydings for "the most scandalous and brazen whitewash of treasonable conspiracy in our history."

By that time, events were moving quickly. On June 25, 1950, seventy-five thousand soldiers from the Democratic People's Republic of Korea (North Korea) crossed the border into the Republic of Korea (South Korea). President Truman thought a line needed to be drawn somewhere against the Communists, and decided Korea was as good a place as any. While several nations sent troops to Korea, the United States supplied a large majority of the soldiers assisting South Korean forces.

Keep in mind that this military attack in Korea came about a year after the fall of China to Communist forces. While the United States government had many issues to consider because of North Korea's invasion, certainly the fall of another nation in Asia to Communists would play into the hands those who believed America was not doing enough to stop the Communist threat. The United States never declared war on North Korea, but its soldiers died there by the thousands regardless of the formalities.

If you added the events of the previous year or so together, it was a frightening time for Americans. There were convicted spies in the government, confessed foreign agents in the nuclear bomb program, and a Communist military effort that already had claimed China and was trying to do the same in South Korea. There's little wonder why so many people bought what McCarthy was selling with his words and tactics.

Back in the United States, those in the entertainment industry once again came under scrutiny. This happened about three years after the Hollywood Ten were blacklisted for their political beliefs. The action was sparked by the publication of a booklet. Roy Brewer, a union leader and a member of the Motion Picture Industry Council, had commissioned a publication called *Red Channels*. The publication was designed to improve the image of the entertainment industry and earned him the nickname of "arbiter of the blacklist." *Red Channels* was written by Ted Kirkpatrick, once an FBI agent, and television producer Vincent Hartnett.

The publication contained 151 names of people who allegedly were members of so-called subversive organizations.

The information came from FBI files, right-wing publications, and the *Daily Worker*, a newspaper put out by the Communist Party in the United States. Copies were sent to top executives in the entertainment industry, and many were blacklisted until they agreed to appear before a Congressional hearing.

FBI Director J. Edgar Hoover, whom you may remember from the first Red Scare, was quoted in the introduction to *Red Channels*. "The [Communist] Party has departed from depending on the written word as its medium of propaganda and has taken to the air. Its members and sympathizers have not only infiltrated the airways but they are now persistently seeking radio channels ... Those familiar with show business are already sickeningly aware of the manner in which Red Fascism has exploited scores of radio and TV stars at pro-Soviet rallies, meetings and conferences."

The names of those in the book included musicians, actors, writers, and composers. The list included Leonard Bernstein, Lee J. Cobb, Aaron Copland, John Garfield, Howard Da Silva, Dashiell Hammett, Lillian Hellman, Burl Ives, Burgess Meredith, Zero Mostel, Arthur Miller, Dorothy Parker, Edward G. Robinson, Pete Seeger, and Orson Welles.

Actress Marsha Hunt was surprised to see her name on the list: "They had listed several affiliations under my name—some I'd never heard about, complete lies. One, I think, had me attending a peace conference in Stockholm. I had never been to Stockholm, nor to a peace conference. The rest were innocent activities that *Red Channels* viewed with suspicion." But she had protested the original HUAC hearings into the entertainment business, and the listing in *Red Channels* essentially ended her career.

The publication had an impact. Laurence Johnson, a food market owner in Syracuse, New York, was ready to place signs in his store windows telling customers not to support broadcast programs that used one of "Stalin's little creatures." His action had a surprisingly large effect on companies that sponsored radio and television broadcasts. Actress Lee Grant lost her acting job on a television soap opera because of Johnson's campaign.

The financial backers of *Red Channels* also ran an operation that would conduct security checks for companies. For $5,000, the staff would investigate employees' names against their files for possible loyalty issues. "The guys who came to see us said if we subscribed to their service, they'd clear everyone we called, so this whole business of clearing people was a blackmailing scheme," said Ira Skutch, a television director and producer.

Bipartisan Persecution

The search for Communists in American society was not restricted to Republicans, as some Democrats also took part. A prominent one was Senator Pat McCarran of Nevada, who after World War II became one of the leading anti-Communists in Congress. He created the Senate Internal Security Subcommittee to investigate members of the Roosevelt and Truman Administrations.

McCarran played his biggest role in September of 1950, when he sponsored the McCarran Internal Security Act. The bill ordered Communist organizations to register with the Department of Justice, authorized the deportation

Investigative reporters Jack Anderson and Drew Pearson often criticized Senator
Joseph McCarthy for his tactics.

of Communists, and tightened immigration laws. President Truman vetoed the bill, saying it was "the greatest danger to freedom of speech, press, and assembly since the Alien and Sedition Laws of 1798." Democrats joined Republicans to override the veto and make the bill a law on September 23.

In the elections of 1950, Republicans who exploited the anti-Communism issue did well. Everett Dirksen won in Illinois and Richard Nixon was victorious in California. Democrat Tydings lost in Maryland. The rest of 1950 was relatively quiet. Still, McCarthy was a participant in one incident that certainly created some news. After all, a senator doesn't strike a newspaper columnist very often.

There are no writers in Washington, DC, like Drew Pearson any more. He was a political columnist who more or less jumped between reporting on the news of the day and trying to influence it through his connections with politicians. Pearson started a column called Washington Merry-Go-Round in 1932, and it continues in syndication to this day.

Pearson had some major scoops in his day. He was the first to report that General George Patton had slapped one of his soldiers in a hospital in the middle of World War II, a story that caused trouble for Patton. After World War II, Pearson was a loud critic of Secretary of Defense James Forrestal, calling for his dismissal. Pearson's assistant, Jack Anderson, later said that some of Pearson's attacks were unfair.

Pearson saved some of his most controversial work for McCarthy. He frequently criticized the Wisconsin Senator in his syndicated newspaper column and made similar comments on his radio show. McCarthy, never one to back down from a fight, went to the Senate and responded in seven speeches. The attacks by the then-popular McCarthy took a toll in the form of cancellation of sponsorships for Pearson's work. McCarthy also is said to have helped with the legal costs for those who wished to sue Pearson, who was cleared in every libel case.

They never should have been invited into the same room socially. Yet that's what happened on the night of December 13, 1950. A party was staged in the Sulgrave Club, a converted millionaire's mansion in the midst of Embassy Row in Washington. The two men agreed that Pearson approached McCarthy, and the two men talked. Then their stories differ.

McCarthy told the Associated Press: "I smacked him with my open hand and knocked him down on his hips. I didn't punch him." Pearson said: "The senator kicked me twice in the groin. As usual he hit below the belt. But his pugilistic powers are about as ineffective as his Senate speeches."

The ugly situation came to an end when another party guest broke up the confrontation. That guest was Nixon. The next day, McCarthy described Pearson as "the diabolically clever voice of international Communism and a Moscow-directed character assassin."

As 1950 drew to a close, the Communist Party of the United States was shrinking. The Congress of Industrial Organizations (CIO), a group of labor unions, expelled about a dozen of its member organizations that were led by Communist Party members. That reduced the organization's influence on the labor movement greatly. Meanwhile, joining the Communists seemed like a way to commit career suicide.

Trial of the Century

The year 1951 was calmer, but it was noteworthy for one particular event. The phrase "trial of the century" is overused, but it could be applied to describe the case of Julius and Ethel Rosenberg. They were, in a sense, two of the few actual casualties of the Red Scare—just like Sacco and Vanzetti, who had died in the 1920s.

Julius Rosenberg was born in New York City on May 12, 1918. He joined the Young Communist League in 1936, where he met a woman named Ethel Greenglass. She wanted to be an actress and a singer, but took a job for a shipping company as a secretary. Greenglass was involved in labor disputes there, and joined the League. They were married in 1939.

Julius became a member of the US Army in 1940 and worked in the Army Signal Corps. In 1942, both Rosenbergs joined the American Communist Party, but they dropped out of that organization a year later. Julius thought he could be more help to the Communists as a spy. His loyalty to the Soviet Union remained strong. Meanwhile, acquaintances said Ethel was too busy raising the family's two sons to spend much time thinking about politics and spying.

Rosenberg's Communist beliefs had been discovered through a connection to Klaus Fuchs, the British scientist who worked on the atomic bomb project in Los Alamos, New Mexico. Intelligence experts had branded Fuchs a spy after the United States broke the Soviet code for secret messages (the Verona Project). Sergeant David Greenglass— Ethel's younger brother—had worked as a machinist at Los

Ethel and Julius Rosenberg were executed for passing secrets to the Soviet Union.

Alamos, and the American intelligence agents followed the trail to David Greenglass from Fuchs. Greenglass confessed to passing secrets along to the Soviets as well, and said he worked with his wife Ruth and Julius Rosenberg, his brother-in-law. Julius was arrested in June 1950, and was defiant at the time. "Bring him here—I'll call him a liar to his face," he told agents. Ethel Rosenberg was arrested about two months later. She wasn't even given time to provide for the care of her two sons, who were being watched by a neighbor.

Some believed that the case against Ethel was less than convincing, and that her arrest had more to do with attempting to coerce her husband to fully confess and supply additional information. Greenglass said Ethel had been present for certain conversations about secret information and that she typed notes.

The trial opened on March 6, 1951, in New York. Remember the times: America was nervous about the spread of Communism, and the nation had lost its nuclear monopoly when the Soviet Union exploded an atomic bomb in 1949 — perhaps in part due to leaks by traitors. No wonder attorney Irving Saypol, who worked on the Alger Hiss case, said the Rosenbergs, along with fellow suspect Morton Sobell, "have committed the most serious crime which can be committed against the people of this country."

Several participants in the case were called, including David Greenglass and wife Ruth, and they outlined the series of events that led to the charges. Once the prosecution was done, the defense called only Julius and Ethel Rosenberg. Julius frequently pled the Fifth Amendment — which protects a witness from having to supply damaging information about himself at his own trial, and thus becoming a witness for the prosecution. He also denied participation in several of the events outlined earlier in the trial. Meanwhile, Ethel followed her husband's lead and also denied any personal connection to spying.

The trial took about a month, and the jury didn't take very long to decide its verdict. One member of the jury was worried about what would happen to the Rosenbergs' children once Ethel was executed, but eventually that juror put such concerns aside. All three defendants, including Sobell, were found guilty.

Judge Irving Kaufman said that the Rosenbergs' crime was "worse than murder" and somehow blamed the two of them for fifty thousand American deaths that had taken place in Korea. Julius and Ethel received the death penalty via electric chair, while Sobell was given a thirty-year jail sentence. Appeals to the verdict were set in motion immediately, as their attorneys worked to prevent the Rosenbergs from becoming a casualty of the age.

Conflict Over Korea

Elsewhere, Senator McCarthy provided a footnote to one of the most famous events of the Korean conflict, which took place shortly after the completion of the Rosenberg Trial. General Douglas MacArthur, the head of American forces in Korea who had been the leader of the US effort in the Pacific in World War II, had said late in 1950 that there was no chance that the Chinese would enter into the conflict. Less than two months later, many thousands of troops from China crossed the border into North Korea to join in the fighting. It was, essentially, an entirely new war.

MacArthur asked Truman for permission to bomb locations in China and expand the war. Truman said no, and the two men grew further apart. In April 1951, Truman fired MacArthur— a move that shocked the nation—and replaced him with General Matthew Ridgway. In an address to the nation, Truman said it "would be wrong—tragically wrong—for us to take the initiative in extending the war … Our aim is to avoid the spread of the conflict." General MacArthur was dismissed, Truman added, "so that there would be no doubt or confusion as to the real purpose and aim of our policy."

The move was not a popular one. MacArthur was a war hero. One poll said MacArthur had the support of 69 percent of the American public in the dispute. Meanwhile, Truman's overall approval rating sank to 23 percent that month. It never reached 40 percent for the rest of his presidency.

McCarthy quickly added a public statement on the situation. McCarthy, no friend or supporter of Secretary of State Dean Acheson, said, "Truman is surrounded by the Jessups, the Achesons, the old Hiss crowd. Most of the tragic things are done at 1:30 and 2 o'clock in the morning when they've had time to get the President cheerful."

It was typical of the relationship, or lack of one, between McCarthy and Acheson. McCarthy frequently charged Acheson with having Communists in the state department, and the senator believed the cabinet member was partly responsible for the "loss" of China. Acheson was a smart, extremely confident person who had good credentials in the Cold War against the Soviets. He played a key role in the formation of the North Atlantic Treaty Organization (NATO) in 1949. Acheson also sided with Truman when it came to MacArthur's firing. The secretary of state found it easy to ignore McCarthy's attacks.

The secretary of defense, George Marshall, wasn't so thick skinned. Marshall's patriotic credentials were as good as anyone's in the United States. He was army chief of staff during World War II and served as secretary of state and secretary of defense under Truman. It was Marshall who came up with the aid program for Europe that saved countless lives and kept some nations from turning to Communism.

Yet McCarthy frequently attacked Marshall. McCarthy took to the Senate floor on June 14, 1951, and viciously charged Marshall with a long list of offenses, including the loss of China to the Communists. The senator went on to accuse the secretary of defense of "having made common cause with Stalin" in "a conspiracy so immense and an infamy so black as to dwarf any such venture in the history of man."

Truman decided not to respond to McCarthy's remarks. McCarthy did take some criticism from Democrats and the media, but he still found receptive audiences when he made similar comments around the country. Marshall was seventy years old at this point, and he no longer had the stomach to fight that sort of criticism. Tired of the politics that came with his job and battling some health issues, he retired later in 1951. Marshall received the Nobel Peace Prize in 1953 for his humanitarian work in Europe after World War II.

Meanwhile, the House Un-American Activities Committee (HUAC) went back to its public work in 1951, as it had waited for the various appeals of the Hollywood Ten to play out. Several people from the entertainment industry appeared as "friendly witnesses," as they identified people they believed had connections to the Communist Party. Writer Richard Collins gave the name of Budd Schulberg, and Schulberg responded by naming others.

Schulberg's popularity within certain segments of Hollywood no doubt suffered because of that action, but he was allowed to continue working in the entertainment business. Schulberg is best known for writing the script to the movie *On the Waterfront,* considered a classic with a memorable performance by actor Marlon Brando. One of its themes was the importance of telling authorities about corruption, no matter who was involved or who was damaged. The director of that film was Elia Kazan, a former member of the Communist Party who identified others before Congress.

War Hero Enters Race

Politics dominated 1952, and the race for the presidency dominated politics. Even though the Constitution had been amended to limit a President's time in office to two terms (this includes any term of more than two years when replacing an elected president), Truman was exempted from the law. However, he opted to not run for office again. That opened up the race considerably, especially on the Democratic side. Senator Estes Kefauver of Tennessee had the most delegates entering the summer convention, but not enough to lock up the nomination. Senator Adlai Stevenson of Illinois, who had turned down requests to run for president earlier in the year, caught the attention of the delegates with a welcoming speech at the start of the convention and won the nomination.

His opponent was something of a surprise. General Dwight Eisenhower was one of the most popular men in the United States after guiding his country's troops to victory in Europe in World War II. Victorious generals sometimes have used their military career as a springboard to political office. Eisenhower had not told anyone whether he was a Democrat or Republican until 1951, when he announced that he was a Republican. Supporters told Eisenhower that it was his duty

War hero Dwight Eisenhower was an easy winner in the 1952 presidential election.

to run for president, and that appealed to him. He left a job with NATO to become a full-time candidate.

At the Republican convention that summer, McCarthy's conclusion to a speech was mentioned in summaries of his life for years to come: "I say one Communist in a defense plant is one too many. One Communist on the faculty of one university is one Communist too many. One Communist among the American advisers at Yalta was one Communist too many. And even if there were one Communist in the State Department, that would still be one Communist too many."

Eisenhower won the presidential nomination and picked Richard Nixon as his running mate in order to shore up his anti-Communist credentials, which was necessary to keep parts of the party happy. On the campaign trail that fall, Eisenhower's path crossed with McCarthy's.

Under Suspicion

Minority groups often have often suffered persecution from the majority of a population in a region or country. At times, large segments of those groups suffered on a personal level from that persecution. Millions of Jews died in Nazi Germany, and an estimated 160,000 Jews and thousands of Muslims were exiled during the Spanish Inquisition.

Actions against the Communists in the United States were of a different type and scale of persecution. A Communist who lived in America between 1917 and 1991 was relatively safe from problems if he simply kept his opinions to himself. Yes, that's a loss of free speech in a sense, something that goes against the principles of the Constitution. But it's a rather light punishment compared to the persecution of other groups.

But there were exceptions. The life story of Owen Lattimore is instructive in teaching us what can happen when someone is placed in unexpected circumstances.

Lattimore was born in China, and was a scholar of Chinese history. He worked with the Chinese government before World War II. At one point, Lattimore wrote "the savagery of the Japanese assault is doing more to spread Communism than the teaching of the Chinese Communists themselves or the influences of Russia."

After the war, China fell to the Communists, and part of a scared America wondered who was responsible. Lattimore was one of the targets—particularly since he thought Chinese leader Chiang Kai-shek could have done much more to install

reforms and hold off the Communist uprising.

Senator Joseph McCarthy said he had evidence that one member of the State Department was clearly a Communist spy, and Lattimore was that person. Soon McCarthy became more specific, forcing the diplomat and author to defend himself in Congress. Lattimore did so ("I believe in my right to be wrong, and still more in my right to be right," he said.), and was cleared of charges. But in 1951–1952, the Senate Internal Security Subcommittee tried again to prosecute Lattimore, who indicated that he had given Congress some minor inaccuracies during his previous testimony. That was enough for the committee to charge him with perjury, although those charges were dropped for technical reasons.

Even so, Lattimore's career certainly was damaged. He turned to the academic world, working at Johns Hopkins University until 1963 and at the University of Leeds until he retired in 1970. Lattimore died in 1989.

Some who have studied the matter believe Lattimore was a Communist spy, while others say he was nothing of the sort. He denied that charge throughout his life. Either way, Lattimore's life changed forever when he became caught up in America's fervor over Communists.

Every Republican was thrilled at the prospect of appearing in public with the popular Eisenhower, McCarthy included. However, George Marshall had been Eisenhower's boss during World War II, and Marshall had played a key role in Eisenhower's rise in the army. Eisenhower resented McCarthy's words and tactics. Eisenhower came to Milwaukee for a campaign appearance and planned to have a paragraph praising Marshall in his speech there. His advisors told him not to include it, as it would reflect poorly on him if he appeared to be criticizing McCarthy, a fellow Republican, in McCarthy's home state. Eisenhower took the paragraph out of the speech, a move he regretted for the rest of his life.

No matter what happened that day, it wasn't going to alter the election's outcome. Eisenhower trounced Stevenson to win the White House, and McCarthy won reelection with about 54 percent of the vote—well below what Eisenhower's winning margin was in Wisconsin. While the Republicans had won their first presidential election since 1928, McCarthy wasn't about to back down on his anti-Communism campaign, even though many had grown weary after three years of listening to him make charges he couldn't prove. Eisenhower once called him "a pimple on the path of progress."

When 1953 arrived, McCarthy was in his second term as a senator, and he thus moved up the seniority list. He was named the chairman of Senate Committee on Government Operations, a harmless–sounding title. However, there was a subcommittee that dealt with investigations, and McCarthy soon realized he could use that legislative body as a tool for his own agenda.

Choreographer and director Jerome Robbins testified to HUAC that he was a member of the Communist Party from 1944 to 1947.

Target number one was the Voice of America, the broadcast service for the **United States Information Agency**. No Communist influence was found despite tough questioning by McCarthy, but morale in the organization dropped and one engineer committed suicide.

In April, McCarthy aides Roy Cohn and David Schine took a seven-country tour of State Department libraries in Europe and claimed thirty thousand books in them were written by pro-Communist writers. The books in question were either removed or burned. It led to efforts to censor or remove books from libraries in the United States, which drew a response from President Eisenhower: "Don't join the book burners … Don't be afraid to go in your library and read every book."

Some events certainly worked in McCarthy's favor that year. In June, Julius and Ethel Rosenberg's legal options finally ran out, and they were executed for espionage. Appeals had been rejected by Presidents Truman and Eisenhower along the way. Ethel Rosenberg was the first woman executed by the United States government since Mary Surratt was hanged for her role in the assassination of Abraham Lincoln. In October, J. Robert Oppenheimer, who had been called "the father of the atomic bomb," lost his security clearance from the Atomic Energy Commission. HUAC continued its investigation of the entertainment business. Some of the friendly witnesses were Jerome Robbins, the choreographer who produced *West Side Story*, and Lee J. Cobb, the star of Elia Kazan's theatrical production of *Death of a Salesman*.

Uneasy Time

The fall of 1953 was certainly a difficult time to be an American who had any connection to Communism. This "Red Scare" wasn't a one-year phenomenon, as it had been in 1919 after World War I. This was at six years and counting. While the people who had been accused of public ties to Communism were limited to only a few groups, certainly others wondered if the spotlight would be turned in their direction in the near future—and they might have to choose between naming other people and committing professional suicide. Membership rolls in the Communist Party were dropping quickly.

Still, there were other events in 1953 that showed that different times might be ahead. One was the death of Soviet leader Joseph Stalin in March. No one knew if one of the most evil men in human history had died of natural causes or was killed by some sort of conspiracy. What was certain was his passing meant that a new era was about to begin in the Soviet Union—and in Communism.

In addition, the Korean conflict came to an end in that summer. After several dramatic battles and developments, the conflict eventually settled into a stalemate. Negotiations dragged on for several months, but finally all sides agreed to stop fighting. A formal peace treaty was never signed. Very little territory changed hands, and many thousands of people died in those three years. But a Communist country's attempt to expand into South Korea had been stopped. That might have made some people consider the possibility that the expansion of Communism wasn't inevitable after all.

Then again, maybe the biggest change might have come from McCarthy himself. People who crave attention must become louder and bolder in their claims in order to continue to stay relevant. By the end of 1953, McCarthy had been riding the anti-Communist movement to fame for almost four years.

Pehaps it was inevitable that the more people saw of the senator from Wisconsin, the more they would become tired of his act.

FOUR

Decline and Fall

Senator Joseph McCarthy's hunt for Communists for three and one-half years had concentrated on strong liberals, government workers, and intellectuals. Some essentially cheered McCarthy on in this period. There was not a reservoir of good feelings toward those groups, particularly among conservatives in the United States. But then McCarthy, through his Senate subcommittee, began a long investigation into Communists in the United States Army.

This was a different matter. Late in 1953, America was about eight years from the end of World War II, and only a few months from the ceasefire in Korea. The army had helped defeat Germany and Japan in the first war and had stopped Communist expansion in the second. What's more, many families had some sort of connection to a person who had been in the military. If they didn't, they probably lived on the same block with an ex-soldier. And the most popular soldier of them all, General Dwight Eisenhower, was now occupying the White House. McCarthy should have known

Opposite: **The television cameras became a large part of the story during the Army-McCarthy hearings of 1954.**

that he was playing with fire here, and it would be relatively easy to lose Middle America on this issue.

Nevertheless, he plunged forward. In October 1953, McCarthy launched an investigation into the Army Signal Corps at Fort Monmouth in New Jersey. Many of the workers there leaned to the left politically. Even though the government had given staff members there a recent and thorough security check, McCarthy pressed ahead with his investigation—and got nowhere. He eventually gave up and moved on.

In January 1954, McCarthy called hearings over a routine promotion of Captain Irving Peress, who had cited the Fifth Amendment when leaving some items unanswered on a questionnaire. During the investigation, General Ralph Zwicker—Peress's commanding officer—declined to answer some questions on the advice of lawyers. McCarthy said General Zwicker had the intelligence of "a five-year-old child," and protected Communists. The senator went after Secretary of the Army Robert Stevens so vigorously that Stevens offered to resign. McCarthy's public image was damaged by the severity of these attacks.

Around this time, a new and crucial element entered the story: television. Radio with pictures had been developed during the 1930s, but its development was put on hold through World War II. By the late 1940s, a regular broadcast schedule was beamed out to an admittedly select group of viewers. As technology improved—making television sets cheaper and broadcasts available to most parts of the country—many people could see that television was going to play a key role in our cultural future.

Edward R. Murrow is considered to be the first great broadcast journalist, covering his time in radio and television.

News had been a big part of radio broadcasting, and it made the transition to television. The biggest name in radio news of that era was Edward R. Murrow, who was famous for his broadcasts out of London during World War II. After working as an executive after the war, Murrow returned to the airwaves and in 1951 was named as the host of a new program called *See It Now*. The show aired news documentaries, and it became the first of the so-called newsmagazines and a predecessor of *60 Minutes*.

On March 9, 1954, Murrow and producer Fred Friendly came after McCarthy with every bit of ammunition they could find. The broadcast used images and sounds of McCarthy presenting half-truths and false charges. It was the ending of the broadcast, though—an opinion-filled conclusion by the host—that will be remembered forever.

"This is no time for men who oppose Senator McCarthy's methods to keep silent, or for those who approve. We can deny our heritage and our history, but we cannot escape responsibility for the result," Murrow said. "The actions of the junior senator from Wisconsin have caused alarm and dismay amongst our allies abroad, and given considerable comfort to our enemies. And whose fault is that? Not really his. He didn't create this situation of fear; he merely exploited it—and rather successfully. Cassius was right: 'The fault, dear Brutus, is not in our stars, but in ourselves.' Good night, and good luck."

McCarthy was offered airtime to respond to the charges, and he quickly did so. He attacked Murrow's own record. At one point, McCarthy said, "Murrow is a symbol, the leader, and the cleverest of the jackal pack which is always found at the throat of anyone who dares to expose individual Communists and traitors."

Some commentators stated that Murrow's accusations about McCarthy had been made by print journalists in the previous several months. They missed the point. Television had given viewers the chance to watch McCarthy in action, and they didn't like what they saw in many cases. The senator's popularity continued to plunge.

McCarthy obviously didn't learn his lesson quickly. Only a couple of weeks after the *See It Now* broadcast, the Senate subcommittee voted to allow television networks to broadcast hearings into actions taken by the senator. The army had accused McCarthy of blackmail, as a McCarthy aide, Roy Cohn, promised to "wreck the army" if it did not give a promotion to one of his aides, the just-drafted David Schine.

The tables were about to be turned on McCarthy. The hearings began on April 22. This time, McCarthy was on the defensive. He made threats against perceived enemies and opponents, and talked endlessly. There were fifty-four sessions at which thirty-two witnesses spoke two million words. Perhaps the most noteworthy statistic was this: The ABC network and Dumont Network broadcast all 187 hours of the hearings. The ratings were enormous—68 percent of all televisions turned on in New York were tuned into the hearings.

The most memorable moment of those 187 hours came on June 9. One of the army's lawyers was Joseph Welch. He had been restrained and dignified during his moments in the spotlight. Welch challenged Cohn to supply the names of the

Joseph Welch's stinging attack on Senator Joseph McCarthy marked a turning point in McCarthy's influence.

Communists and spies who were working at Fort Monmouth in New Jersey. McCarthy came back at Welch later that day with a charge that a member of Welch's law firm had belonged to the National Lawyers Guild, which had been called a front for a Communist group. He did this even though the two sides had previously agreed not to bring up the man's political history.

Welch responded to the moment: "Until this moment, Senator, I think I never really gauged your cruelty, or your recklessness." He soon added, "Little did I dream you could be so reckless and so cruel as to do an injury to that lad. It

Kennan and Containment

George F. Kennan ranks as one of the most important figures in the history of the United States in the twentieth century, even if he remains relatively unknown.

Born in 1904, Kennan joined the US Foreign Service after graduating from Princeton. He served in several posts in Europe and became an expert on the Soviet Union. Kennan became disenchanted with the Soviets over time, eventually calling them an unfit ally even before the United States entered World War II.

After the war, Kennan was stationed in Moscow. He sent a long essay to the State Department that urged the United States to build up its institutions in an effort to contain the worldwide expansion of Soviet influence. That went against US policy of working with the USSR. Kennan expanded those ideas in an anonymous magazine article in 1947. This diplomatic approach came to be known as "containment," and it became the foundation for US policy for decades.

Some historians say Kennan's finest moment came in May 1953, as he attacked Senator Joe McCarthy in a rare public speech: "I have the deepest misgivings about the direction and effects of their efforts. In general, I feel what they are doing is unwise and unfortunate, and I am against it. They distort and exaggerate the dimensions of the problem with which they profess to deal." That took courage, as McCarthy was at the height of his popularity.

On the list of Americans who helped win the Cold War, Kennan is near the top.

is, I regret to say, equally true that I fear he shall always bear a scar needlessly inflicted by you. If it were in my power to forgive you for your reckless cruelty, I would do so. I like to think I'm a gentle man, but your forgiveness will have to come from someone other than me." And when McCarthy continued to press the issue, Welch replied, "You've done enough. Have you no sense of decency, sir, at long last? Have you left no sense of decency?"

That moment ranked as the turning point in the decline of McCarthy's influence. Once he had been exposed in public, on national television, as a bully, his public life would never be the same. McCarthy's only consolation was that he was cleared of the original charges from the army, in part because Republicans controlled the committee.

Still, talk of a Red Scare didn't immediately disappear. It's something of a historical coincidence that President Eisenhower signed a law changing the Pledge of Allegiance less than a week after the moment involving Welch and McCarthy. Before this action, the Pledge read "one nation, indivisible, with liberty and justice for all." Now it read "one nation under God, indivisible, with liberty and justice for all." The change was made to illustrate the difference between the government of the United States and those countries under what was called "Godless Communism."

Legislators and judges were busy that year. Congress passed the Communist Control Act. This law was a bit vague, but it established penalties for Communist organizations that didn't register the names of their supporters with the federal government. While the bill hinted that the Communist Party

Joseph McCarthy was censured by a vote of the United States Senate in 1954. Senate Resolution 301 stated his actions were "contrary to senatorial traditions."

itself should be outlawed and that membership would be punished by a fine or jail sentence, a complete ban never was enforced—perhaps because of constitutional issues. The legislation was more of a political document than a legal one, as lawmakers were anxious to show voters that they were doing something to fight Communism.

Congress also passed a law that would take away American citizenship from anyone who was found guilty of trying to overthrow the US government by force. States were requiring loyalty oaths from their employees, and the death penalty became the new punishment for espionage during peacetime. The Supreme Court also ruled that aliens could be deported for being a member of the Communist Party.

But McCarthy's influence was dropping quickly. On June 11, two days after the Welch incident, Vermont senator Ralph Flanders introduced a resolution that would disqualify McCarthy from serving as the head of any Senate committee. A total of forty-six charges eventually were added to the resolution. Hearings began on August 31 and lasted for about two months. The number of charges was reduced to two: failure to cooperate with other members of the Subcommittee on Rules and Administration along with abuse of its members, and McCarthy's abuse of General Zwicker. The latter charge was replaced when the full Senate considered the measure. The vote was on whether McCarthy "acted contrary to senatorial ethics and tended to bring the Senate into dishonor and disrepute, to obstruct the constitutional processes of the Senate, and to impair its dignity."

The 67–22 vote to condemn McCarthy came on December 2. Forty-four Democrats and one independent voted against McCarthy, while forty-four Republicans were evenly split. Short of kicking someone out of the Senate completely, a censure or condemnation is the biggest weapon the Senate has to express disapproval of actions. It's been done nine times in American history.

Soviet spies were a problem in the United States from 1945 to 1950, and McCarthy had a chance to perform a public service. However, his investigations were so poorly conducted (none of those investigated went to prison) that he damaged his own credibility. McCarthy also did not change his tactics and targets once Eisenhower took office in 1953, making the senator unpopular with both parties. It was just a matter of time from that point until his downfall.

As Eisenhower put it, "It's no longer McCarthyism. It's McCarthywasm."

FIVE

Irrelevance

The effects of "McCarthyism" lasted longer than Joseph McCarthy.

McCarthy stayed in the Senate after his condemnation, but he had little impact. His speeches were usually given in an empty chamber. McCarthy still traveled the country in search of friendly audiences, and his anti-Communist views were presented at those times. However, his remarks were no longer news and were generally ignored. McCarthy had fought problems with alcohol, and they became worse after the Senate's action. He eventually was diagnosed with cirrhosis of the liver. McCarthy died on May 2, 1957, and he is buried in Appleton, Wisconsin.

Robert Kennedy, brother of President John Kennedy and later a senator from New York, summed up McCarthy's life this way: "It was so exciting and exhilarating as he went downhill that it didn't matter to him if he hit a tree at the bottom."

Opposite: Earl Warren was one of the most influential chief justices in the history of the Supreme Court.

Meanwhile, the Supreme Court soon became active in chipping away at the legality of some of the actions of McCarthy and his followers through decisions in the next few years. This happened in part because of two of Eisenhower's appointments to the court who turned out to be much more liberal than they were first thought: Earl Warren and William Brennan.

Harry Slochower was a Brooklyn College teacher who pleaded the Fifth Amendment when asked about membership in the Communist Party. The school board took that as admission of guilt. He was fired from his position. In *Slochower v. Board of Higher Education of New York City*, the Supreme Court ruled in 1956 that the Fifth Amendment wouldn't have much value if someone could lose a job simply by citing it in court.

In *Yates v. United States*, the court ruled in 1957 on the case in which fourteen members of the Communist Party were charged with violating the Smith Act, which established penalties for calling for the overthrow of the government. The conviction was overturned, as the majority of the justices ruled that simply being a Communist Party member and believing that a new form of government should be used was different than actually calling for that action.

John Watkins was convicted for refusing to answer questions from members for the House Un-American Activities Committee, which wanted to know about people whom he believed were no longer members of the Communist Party. The Supreme Court ruled in 1957 in *Watkins v. United States* that Watkins had not received legal protection under the due process clause of the Constitution and overturned his contempt of Congress conviction.

Rockwell Kent had his passport application turned down because of alleged connections to the Communist Party. Kent was told he had to appear at a hearing on the case and sign a document attesting to whether he had ever been a Communist. Kent refused and was not given a passport. The Supreme Court ruled in 1958 that one of the foundations of liberty is the right to travel freely. While certain restrictions were allowed, the complete ban of such trips was in conflict with the Constitution.

If we call 1958 the end of the era of McCarthyism, let's summarize the scope of its effects numerically. Most basic rights were still in effect. No American went to trial without a lawyer, and no American went to jail without a trial. Historians estimate that about ten thousand people lost their jobs for "political reasons." About two thousand of those ten thousand worked for the government. Only forty of the dismissals had a direct connection to McCarthy himself. Fewer than a dozen people overall were convicted of espionage, and only two—the Rosenbergs on June 19, 1953—were executed. It's clear that people were targeted selectively. However, the fearful atmosphere during that time, which lingered in some ways, should not be discounted.

"I am more than a little disquieted that McCarthy's condemnation by the Senate and his subsequent death have satisfied so many people that McCarthyism is over," said Raymond Swing, a former employee of the Voice of America. "I feel that it left out of its account in its condemnation most

Easy Target

Paul Robeson was a target of McCarthyism for many reasons. He was a political activist, an outspoken African American, and an admitted Communist. He was also a man of immense and varied talents. At Rutgers University, he earned fifteen varsity letters in baseball, track, football, and basketball, then graduated as class valedictorian. After playing pro football, he earned a law degree. When a secretary refused to take dictation from a black man, he left the practice of law and started acting. He starred in films and plays, including the musical *Showboat*. He toured Europe as a singer and spoke out for equality for all people. His political stances made him unpopular in the United States, and in 1950 the State Department revoked his passport. This harmed his ability to earn a living.

According to the National Archives, Robeson said to the House Un-American Activities Committee in 1956, "Whether I am or not a Communist is irrelevant. The question is whether American citizens, regardless of their political beliefs or sympathies, may enjoy their constitutional rights." The US Supreme Court ruled in 1958 that political beliefs or affiliations were not proper cause for the State Department to deny citizens the right to travel. However, the damage was done as the travel ban affected his health and ruined his career.

Paul Robeson's Communist ties effectively ruined his career as an entertainer.

of what Senator McCarthy had injuriously done. It ignored his roughshod disregard of civil rights and his irrepressible **mendacity**, and the fact that they existed while he was acting with the authority of the Senate. These transgressions were not specifically and helpfully rebuked at the time or ever. American principles and ethics were not strengthened by the Senate resolution of condemnation ... It simply was rid of a menace because some Senate conservatives realized that their dignity was being sullied."

Let's see what happened to some people connected to that era. Alger Hiss went into private business briefly. In 1975, the "Pumpkin Papers" were revealed to the public after a lawsuit, and they revealed little that could be called incriminating to Hiss. He was soon readmitted to the Massachusetts bar. When the Soviet Union broke up, American authorities asked about Hiss but received conflicting answers. Therefore, we may never reach any final conclusions about his loyalties. Hiss died in 1996.

Similar shadows surround the status of Julius and Ethel Rosenberg. Some of the witnesses in the case have admitted over the years that they lied during their testimony. It seems likely that Julius was involved in some sort of Soviet spy ring. Codefendant Morton Sobell admitted in 2008 that he was an agent, and that Julius helped pass along information. However, Sobell added that none of that information involved important atomic secrets. That fact might have made a difference in sentencing Rosenberg to death. Meanwhile, Sobell said he thought Ethel Rosenberg was aware of what her husband was doing, but that she was not an active participant in the spy ring. **Grand jury** testimony by David Greenglass indicates that he never talked to his sister about espionage activities, and records from the Soviet equivalent to the CIA indicate that Ethel was not an agent.

Perhaps the most interesting case of the aftereffects of Senator McCarthy's four-year period of notoriety centers on one of the men who helped stop it, Edward R. Murrow. The famous broadcast of *See It Now* had only added to his legend as one of the great news broadcasters in history. Less well known was the reaction from his bosses.

CBS was a giant in the news business during the 1950s. The *See It Now* broadcast about McCarthy made a great many people connected to CBS uncomfortable. Executives at the network had a bit of warning that a controversial broadcast was coming, and afterward they were more than happy to accept congratulations from those who were offering them. But sponsors don't like controversy, and neither do television affiliates.

The ratings for *See It Now* were rarely high, and the show's main sponsor, Alcoa, eventually dropped out. The program became an occasional feature on CBS's schedule starting in 1955. In 1958, Murrow made a speech in Chicago charging that television was insulating its audience from reality. The network's news documentaries eventually folded into a program called *CBS Reports*, airing occasionally during the course of 1959–1960. Murrow narrated only some of them.

Murrow's days were about over at CBS. After John F. Kennedy was sworn in as president in January 1961, he picked Murrow to become the head of the United States

Information Agency. Murrow stayed on that job through early 1964, when he resigned because he had lung cancer. The irony there was that See It Now was the first television program to report on the health risks of smoking. Murrow died in 1965 at the age of fifty-seven.

Elsewhere in the entertainment industry, people who had been blacklisted had to use their talents in different ways or disguise their identities in order to keep working. Some members of the Hollywood Ten gave up on show business entirely, switching to writing or teaching. Many wrote under assumed names until the blacklist ended.

As for the Communist Party of the United States, its problems continued to multiply. The membership numbers dropped throughout the 1950s, as it seemed that anyone who even looked into the organization out of curiosity would become the political equivalent of radioactive. The official party newspaper, the Daily Worker, went out of business in 1958 after a run of more than thirty years. Feelings from strong anti-Communists were summed up with the slogan "Better dead than red," as that color often was used as a synonym for Communism.

A pair of events in 1956 didn't help Communists in the United States. In February of that year, Nikita Khrushchev—the new premier of the Soviet Union—gave what came to be called the "Secret Speech." It was a surprise attack on the policies and actions of Joseph Stalin. Khrushchev at one point said, "It is here that Stalin showed in a whole series of cases his intolerance, his brutality, and his abuse of power ... He often chose the path of repression and physical annihilation,

New Soviet leader Nikita Khrushchev's attack on his predecessor Joseph Stalin caused a divide among Communists around the world.

not only against actual enemies, but also against individuals who had not committed any crimes against the party or the Soviet Government."

The speech split Communists throughout the world, with some defending Stalin and others attacking him. That included the party members in the United States. Then came an attempted uprising in Hungary, which was crushed by Soviet forces. The ruthless show of force won no friends in America, including those within the Communist Party.

Eventually, new leadership took control of the party in the United States. Gus Hall frequently toured the country in an attempt to promote his Socialist viewpoints. Hall was the Communist Party candidate for president in 1972, 1976, 1980, and 1984. His vote total peaked in 1976 when he received about fifty-nine thousand votes. The party gave up trying to make an impact on presidential elections after 1984, choosing to concentrate on local elections. It has endorsed Democratic candidates since 1988.

The Communist Party of the United States still exists today. It has called for an immediate move to the political left toward Socialism. The group has tried to align itself with other groups that have progressive goals, such as the gay rights and environmental movements.

The era of McCarthyism may have ended with McCarthy's loss of influence, but the competing sides in the Cold War still created enough incidents to cause concerns among Americans. For example, the Soviet Union launched a spacecraft that orbited Earth on October 4, 1957. It could be seen from the ground and heard on a short-wave radio. The capsule's name was *Sputnik* ("fellow traveler" in Russian). While US government officials weren't surprised by the launch, it did catch the public in the country off guard.

Fears of the Soviet military were still present in the United States, and now the USSR had sent a spacecraft over American territory. It didn't take much of a leap in imagination to picture the Soviets launching missiles that dropped bombs on the United States. America had been working on its own rocket program, and the nation moved into the Space Age the following year with the Vanguard program. It was easy to compare the two space programs as they took their baby steps skyward. President Kennedy later made it a formal race by saying America would put a man on the moon and return him safely by the end of the 1960s. The United States did exactly that in 1969.

Sputnik had two other major effects. It effectively buried the Soviet Union's image as a backward nation, thus scoring points with other countries. The launch also prompted the United States to begin to emphasize math and science in its educational system. That proved to have large benefits for all of American society.

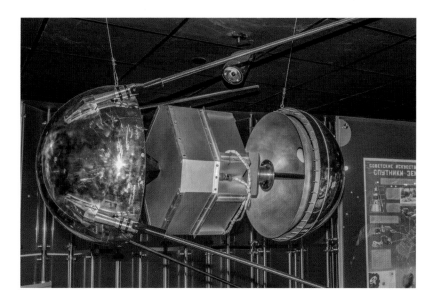

Sputnik was the first spacecraft to orbit Earth. The Soviets launched it in 1957.

If the space race was an interesting part of international competition between the United States and Soviet Union, the arms race was deadly serious. Both sides exploded hydrogen bombs in the 1950s. These devices had many times the power of the atomic bombs that were used on Japan at the end of World War II in 1945. The rivals kept building nuclear weapons to the point where every possible target on each side was covered and destruction of the world was possible. The nuclear arms race reached the point where the use of one atomic bomb would cause a massive response by both sides and there would be nothing left to conquer. The situation was called "mutually assured destruction," or MAD.

The countries did come very close to nuclear war in October 1962. Military planes took pictures of the construction of Soviet missile sites in Cuba—only 90 miles (145 km) from Florida. President Kennedy ordered a blockade of Soviet ships headed to Cuba. The world held its breath while waiting to see how Soviet premier Khrushchev would react. The two sides eventually made a deal in which the missiles would come out of Cuba if the United States pledged not to invade Cuba. That ended the crisis. Later, in another part of that agreement, America removed some of its missiles from Italy and Turkey.

While the Soviet Union added to its conventional (non-nuclear) arsenal in the 1960s and 1970s, the United States—perhaps distracted by its involvement in the Vietnam War and its aftereffects —did not try to keep up. However, President Ronald Reagan came into office in 1981 and began a military buildup. That made the Soviets nervous, as their weak economy made it difficult to counter Reagan's actions. Mikhail Gorbachev, who took over the leadership of the Soviet Union in 1985, tried to shift that country's positions in a number of ways. It was too late; the Soviet Union collapsed in 1991. As Gorbachev said in his farewell address, "The old system collapsed before the new one had time to begin working." Essentially, the United States won the Cold War without firing a shot against the Soviets.

With the Soviet Union now broken up into several smaller countries, the United States ranked as the world's only remaining superpower. America seemed poised to enter another golden age. But everything changed on September 11, 2001. The attacks by radical Muslims on Washington and New York City shocked and scared the United States. The Department of Homeland Security was created, and the Patriot Act was signed into law. Protests that civil liberties had been lost in the process of responding to the attacks soon followed.

America had another frightening enemy who seemingly could strike without warning, and the conversation about what to do about it continued for years. It became a major topic of debate in the presidential campaign of 2016, when Donald Trump proposed banning Muslims from even entering the country.

Once again, we were faced with the question of how a free society deals with outsiders who want to bring harm to America and its citizens. How far must we go to be secure and yet not give up our freedom? We can only look to history for guidance.

Major Events of the Red Scare

March 8–12, 1917: A revolution successfully overthrows the Russian monarchy and replaces it with a provisional government.

November 6–8, 1917: The Bolsheviks take power in Russia.

November 11, 1918: World War I ends.

June 2, 1919: Anarchists set off bombs in seven cities in the United States.

January 2, 1920: Government agents launch "The Palmer Raids," arresting thousands on suspicion of radicalism.

July 14, 1921: Sacco and Vanzetti are convicted of robbery and murder.

June 22, 1941: Germany invades the Soviet Union, breaking a nonaggression pact between the two countries.

December 7, 1941: A Japanese surprise attack on Pearl Harbor brings the United States into World War II against Germany, Japan, and Italy.

August 14, 1945: Japan unconditionally surrenders to end World War II, days after the United States drops atomic bombs on two Japanese cities. Germany had been defeated earlier in the year.

March 5, 1946: Winston Churchill gives his famous Iron Curtain speech in Fulton, Missouri.

June 23, 1947: Congress passes the Taft-Hartley Act, which restricts some activities by labor organizations, over President Truman's veto.

October 20, 1947: The House Un-American Activities Committee (HUAC) begins hearings as part of an investigation into the role of Communists in the entertainment industry.

April 3, 1948: The Marshall Plan, an aid package to European countries, is signed into law.

October 1, 1949: China's government falls to the Communists.

January 21, 1950: Alger Hiss is convicted on two counts of perjury.

January 27, 1950: Klaus Fuchs confesses that he is a Soviet spy during a trial in England. He is sentenced on March 1, 1950.

February 9, 1950: Senator Joseph McCarthy gives a speech in Wheeling, West Virginia, charging that 205 members of the State Department are Communists.

June 25, 1950: North Korean troops invade South Korea, starting a war that would last about three years.

September 23, 1950: The McCarran Internal Security Act, which restricted the civil rights of Communists, goes into effect when both houses of Congress vote to override President Truman's veto.

March 29, 1951: Julius and Ethel Rosenberg are convicted of espionage and sentenced to death via the electric chair.

November 4, 1952: Dwight Eisenhower is elected President of the United States by a landslide over Adlai Stevenson.

March 5, 1953: Joseph Stalin, the premier of the Soviet Union, dies.

July 27, 1953: The Korean War ends as both sides agree to an armistice.

March 9, 1954: *See It Now*, a CBS documentary hosted by Edward R. Murrow, airs a thirty-minute program about Senator Joseph McCarthy. It shows the senator speaking half-truths and making false charges, thus damaging his credibility.

June 9, 1954: Attorney Joseph Welch attacks Senator McCarthy during testimony in the Army-McCarthy Hearings, by saying, "Have you no sense of decency, sir, at long last?"

December 2, 1954: The US Senate condemns Joseph McCarthy.

October 4, 1957: The Soviet Union sends the first man-made satellite, Sputnik, into orbit.

December 26, 1991: The Soviet Union dissolves.

GLOSSARY

anarchist A person who believes government and laws are not necessary.

blacklist A list of people who are viewed suspiciously because of their beliefs or opinions and therefore are not hired for jobs.

buffer zone An area of land that separates neighboring regions. This is often used as a way of reducing potential conflict between nations.

calumny A malicious statement designed to injure a reputation.

civil liberties These are basic rights and freedoms that cannot be taken from individuals. Some are listed in the United States Constitution, while others have been added to the list by Supreme Court decisions.

Cold War An ideological war fought using propaganda, in which overt military action is avoided and diplomatic relations are kept. This conflict between the United States and the USSR lasted for most of the second half of the twentieth century.

The Communist Manifesto Written by Karl Marx and Friedrich Engels, this pamphlet makes the argument that the history of existing society is the history of class struggles, that private property will be abolished, and that the proletariat will rule.

czar The leader of all of Russia from the sixteenth century through 1917. A czarina is the czar's wife.

deported Expelled from a country, usually because of some form of illegal status (for example, illegal entry) or for committing a crime.

due process A phrase in the US Constitution that guarantees that legal proceedings for everyone will follow established rules and principles.

Fourteen Points President Woodrow Wilson's outline for the principles of world peace was presented in a speech to Congress in January 1918.

grand jury A jury authorized by the judicial system to hear evidence about possible criminal conduct and determine if criminal charges should be filed.

inflation An increase in the cost of goods and services. It's often expressed in terms of a percentage over a period of time, such as a year. Inflation decreases the value of currency. For example, a five percent inflation rate in a year would mean one dollar would be worth ninety-five cents in purchasing power a year later.

mendacity A lack of honesty, or a tendency to lie.

sharecropping A farming system in which a landowner allows a tenant to grow crops on the property in return for a share of the products or proceeds.

Socialism An economic system in which portions of property, which includes some businesses, are owned by the nation. Communism believes the state must control all means of production, and also has a strong political aspect that does not include democracy.

Technological Revolution A series of inventions in the late nineteenth century that helped business grow at enormous rates. This covered such developments as railroad networks, the use of the telegraph and telephone, and the commercial use of petroleum products.

United States Information Agency A part of the federal government devoted to public diplomacy. It existed from 1953 to 1999. The best-known part of the agency is the Voice of America, which still supplies information to people around the world through radio, television, and the internet.

warrant This action by a judge or another official allows a law enforcement officer to search private property or to make an arrest, based on information that makes it probable that a particular person committed a certain crime.

the war to end all wars This phrase is interchangeable with "the war to end war," referring to World War I. The latter was a book title for a collection of essays by H. G. Wells published in 1914, and it caught on as a common phrase used to describe the large, multinational conflict.

Books

Dudziak, Mary L. *Cold War Civil Rights: Race and the Image of American Democracy.* Politics and Society in Twentieth-Century America. Princeton, NJ: Princeton University Press, 2011.

Kling, Andrew A. *The Red Scare.* World History Series. Farmington Hills, MI: Lucent Books, 2011.

Woods, Jeff. *Black Struggle, Red Scare: Segregation and Anti-Communism in the South*, 1948–1968. Baton Rouge, LA: LSU Press, 2003.

Films

The Crucible (1996). This is a film adaptation of Arthur Miller's play about the Salem witch trials. The play was written as a critique of the anti-Communist witch hunts.

Dr. Strangelove or: How I Learned to Stop Worrying and Love the Bomb (1964). This classic by Stanley Kubrick spoofs the fanaticism of the Cold War.

Good Luck, and Good Night (2005). This is the story directed by George Clooney of journalist Edward R. Murrow and his attempt to bring down Senator Joseph McCarthy.

Online Articles

Cold War Museum
"Senator Joseph R. McCarthy, McCarthyism, and the Witch Hunt."
http://www.coldwar.org/articles/50s/senatorjosephmccarthy.asp

The Gilder Lehrman Institute of American History
"Anti-Communism in the 1950s"
http://www.gilderlehrman.org/history-by-era/fifties/essays/anti-communism-1950s

History.com
"Joseph R. McCarthy"
http://www.history.com/topics/cold-war/joseph-mccarthy

John F. Kennedy Presidential Library and Museum
"The Cold War"
https://www.jfklibrary.org/JFK/JFK-in-History/The-Cold-War.aspx

Ourdocuments.gov
"Senate Resolution 301: Censure of Senator Joseph McCarthy (1954)
http://www.ourdocuments.gov/doc.php?flash=true&doc=86

SELECTED BIBLIOGRAPHY

Books

Barson, Michael, and Steven Heller. *Red Scared!: The Commie Menace in Propaganda and Popular Culture.* San Francisco, CA: Chronicle, 2001.

Grant, Lee. *I Said Yes to Everything.* New York: Penguin, 2014.

Halbertstam, David. *The Fifties.* New York: Villard, 1993.

Herman, Arthur. *Joseph McCarthy: Reexamining the Life and Legacy of America's Most Hated Senator.* New York: Free Press, 1999.

Murray, Robert K. *Red Scare: A Study in National Hysteria, 1919–1920.* Minneapolis, MN: University of Minnesota Press, 1955.

Schrecker, Ellen. *The Age of McCarthyism: A Brief History with Documents.* Boston, MA: St. Martin's Press, 1994.

Schwartz, Richard A. *The 1950s: An Eyewitness History.* New York: Facts on File, 2003.

Wicker, Thomas. *Shooting Star: The Brief Arc of Joe McCarthy.* Orlando, FL: Harcourt, 2006.

Online Articles

Barnes, Michael. "Joseph McCarthy." United States History. Accessed April 24, 2016. http://www.u-s-history.com/pages/h1774.html.

Barrick, Jessica. "Communism and the Civil Rights Movement of the 1930s." *Commonplaces*, Fall 2011. http://commonplaces. davidson.edu/vol-2/communism-and-the-civil-rights-movement-of-the-1930s.

"Book Burning in History: A Tool of Tyrants." *Homeland Security News Wire*. September 10, 2010. http://www. homelandsecuritynewswire.com/book-burning-history-tool-tyrants.

Burnett, Paul. "The Red Scare." University of Missouri Kansas City. Accessed March 28, 2016. http://law2.umkc.edu/faculty/ projects/ftrials/SaccoV/redscare.html.

Chambers, John Whitclay II. "The McCarran Internal Security Act." Encyclopedia.com. Accessed April 20, 2016. http://www. encyclopedia.com/doc/1O126-TheMcCarranInternlScrtyct.html.

Davies, Richard. "America's Scariest Book? Red Channels." *AbeBooks Book Blog*, February 13, 2009. http://www.abebooks.com/ blog/index.php/2009/02/13/americas-scariest-book-red-channels.

Devinatz, Victor G. "The Communist Party of the United States of America." Britannica.com. Updated December 12, 2014. http:// www.britannica.com/topic/Communist-Party-of-the-United-States-of-America.

Dunbar, David L. "The Hollywood Ten: The Men Who Refused to Name Names." *Hollywood Reporter*, November 16, 2015. http://www.hollywoodreporter.com/lists/hollywood-ten-men-who-refused-839762/item/edward-dmytryk-1908-1999-839784.

"Enemies from Within: Senator Joseph R. McCarthy's Accusations of Disloyalty." History Matters. Accessed April 18, 2016. http://historymatters.gmu.edu/d/6456.

"Expulsion and Censure." United States Senate. Accessed April 27, 2016. http://www.senate.gov/artandhistory/history/common/briefing/Expulsion_Censure.htm.

The Gale Group. "Communist Party USA." Encyclopedia.com. 2005. Accessed April 7, 2016. http://www.encyclopedia.com/topic/Communist_party_%28United_States%29.aspx.

Goldstein, Robert Justin. "Prelude to McCarthyism: The Making of a Blacklist." National Archives, Fall 2006. http://www.archives.gov/publications/prologue/2006/fall/agloso.html.

Herman, Arthur. "Joseph McCarthy." *New York Times*. 1999. Accessed April 27, 2016. http://www.nytimes.com/books/first/h/herman-mccarthy.html

"Julius and Ethel Rosenberg." Atomicarchive.com. Accessed April 22, 2016. http://www.atomicarchive.com/Bios/Rosenberg.shtml.

Kelley, Robin D. G. "The Case of the 'Scottsboro Boys.'" University of Pennsylvania. Accessed April 6, 2016. http://www.writing.upenn.edu/~afilreis/88/scottsboro.html.

Launius, Roger D. "Sputnik and the Origins of the Space Age." NASA. Accessed April 27, 2016. http://history.nasa.gov/sputnik/sputorig.html.

Leviero, Anthony. "Final Vote Condemns M'Carthy, 67-22, for Abusing Senate and Committee." *New York Times*, December 3, 1954. http://www.nytimes.com/learning/general/onthisday/big/1202.html.

Markowitz, Norman. "Budd Schulberg, the Screenwriter Who Named Names, Could Have Been a Contender." *People's World*, August 7, 2009. http://peoplesworld.org/budd-schulberg-screenwriter-who-named-names-could-have-been-a-contender.

"McCarthy-Welch Exchange." American Rhetoric. Speech delivered June 9, 1954. Accessed May 5, 2016. http://www.americanrhetoric.com/speeches/welch-mccarthy.html.

Murrow, Edwin R. "A Report on Senator Joseph McCarthy." See It Now, March 9, 1954. Transcribed July 7, 2006, from *The McCarthy Years*. Accessed April 26, 2016. http://www.lib.berkeley.edu/MRC/murrowmccarthy.html.

"Sacco and Vanzetti." Digital History. Accessed April 7, 2016. http://www.digitalhistory.uh.edu/disp_textbook.cfm?smtID=2&psid=3387.

Shelton, Willard. "Lattimore Case: McCarthy's Vicious Retreat." *The Nation*, April 23, 2009. https://www.thenation.com/article/lattimore-case-mccarthys-vicious-retreat.

"Sputnik Launched." This Day in History. Accessed May 4, 2016. http://www.history.com/this-day-in-history/sputnik-launched.

Storrs, Landon R. Y. "McCarthyism and the Second Red Scare." American History: Oxford Research Encyclopedias, July 2015. http://americanhistory.oxfordre.com/view/10.1093/acrefore/9780199329175.001.0001/acrefore-9780199329175-e-6.

Trueman, C. N. "Russia and World War I." The History Learning Site, May 22, 2015. http://www.historylearningsite.co.uk/modern-world-history-1918-to-1980/russia-1900-to-1939/russia-and-world-war-one.

"Truman Relieves MacArthur of Duties in Korea." This Day in History. Accessed April 24, 2016. http://www.history.com/this-day-in-history/truman-relieves-macarthur-of-duties-in-korea.

Wagner, Steven. "How Did the Taft-Hartley Bill Come About?" History News Network, October 14, 2002. http://historynewsnetwork.org/article/1036.

Weiser, Kathy. "1919 Anarchist Bombings." Legends of America. July 2014. http://www.legendsofamerica.com/ah-1919bombings.html.

Videos

"Arthur Herman: Joseph McCarthy." Booknotes, February 6, 2000. http://www.booknotes.org/Watch/154513-1/Arthur+Herman.aspx.

"Churchill's 'Iron Curtain' Speech." Posted March 7, 2011. https://www.youtube.com/watch?v=S2PUIQpAEAQ.

"Edward R. Murrow: A Report on Senator Joseph R. McCarthy." See It Now, March 9, 1954. Posted November 10, 2014. https://www.youtube.com/watch?v=-YOlueFbG4g.

"Have You No Sense of Decency Sir? Welch-McCarthy." Posted September 4, 2013. https://www.youtube.com/watch?v=K1eA5bUzVjA.

"Keith Hughes: The Palmer Raids Explained: US History Review." Posted April 8, 2014. https://www.youtube.com/watch?v=GhAI9hVAvmk.

"Rosenberg Case." Posted February 11, 2013. https://www.youtube.com/watch?v=IH4_oxjeVVw.

"Senator Joe McCarthy's 'Enemies from Within' Speech." C-Span video, December 16, 2014. http://www.c-span.org/video/?323466-1/senator-joe-mccarthys-enemies-within-speech.

"Senator Joseph McCarthy 1952 Republican Convention." Posted May 30, 2015. https://www.youtube.com/watch?v=8Ul6glasMNc.

Page numbers in **boldface** are illustrations. Entries in **boldface** are glossary terms.

ABOUT THE AUTHOR

Budd Bailey has been a sports reporter and editor at the *Buffalo News* since 1993. Before that, Budd worked for the Buffalo Sabres hockey team and for WEBR Radio. This is Budd's sixth book; he has written biographies of Jackie Robinson and Booker T. Washington for Cavendish Square. Budd and his wife, Jody, live in Buffalo, New York.